Poetry of the Earth:
Trilingual Mapuche Anthology

Edited by Jaime Luis Huenún Villa

Spanish into Mapudungun Translation by
Víctor Cifuentes Palacios

Spanish into English Translation by
Juan Garrido Salgado, Steve Brock and Sergio Holas

Interactive Press
Literature Series

Interactive Press
an imprint of Interactive Publications
Treetop Studio • 9 Kuhler Court
Carindale, Queensland, Australia 4152
sales@ipoz.biz
ipoz.biz/IP/IP.htm

First published by IP, 2014
© Jaime Luis Huenún Villa and IP, 2014

Printed in 12 pt Cochin on Charlemagne Std 12pt.

National Library of Australia Cataloguing-in-Publication entry:

Title: Poetry of the Earth: trilingual Mapuche anthology / Jaime Luis Huenún Villa (editor) ; Mapudungun translator, Víctor Cifuentes Palacios ; translation into English, Juan Garrido Salgado, Steve Brock and Sergio Holas ; contributors, Bernardo Colipán, Maribel Mora Curriao, Omar Huenuqueo Huaiquinao, Paulo Huirimilla, María Isabel Lara Millapán, Roxana Miranda Rupailaf, Jaime Luis Huenún Villa.

ISBN: 9781922120175 (paperback)

Subjects: Mapuche poetry.

Dewey Number: 898.72

Acknowledgements

Cover Art: Eduardo Rapimán Marín, *Niña y Tierra* (acrílico sobre tela, 2003)

Book design: David P Reiter

Thank you to Graham Rowlands for revising the English versions of the poems, and to Luis González Serrano for his comments on the translations from Spanish to English. Thank you also to Chris Ingleton and Geoff Goodfellow for reading the manuscript and providing editorial advice.

A special thank you to David Reiter for editorial advice and taking on this brave publishing venture.

For first publication of English translations in this anthology, grateful acknowledgement is made to *Cordite*, *Famous Reporter* and *Rabbit*.

Contents

Foreword

Poetry of the Earth: Trilingual Mapuche Anthology reflects the many challenges facing colonised Indigenous peoples of the world and the tactics of freedom struggle used to meet these challenges.

As a dispossessed Aborigine in Australia, I have seen too much violence, too many deaths in custody and far too many western schools failing our children.

Whether it be the continued colonial presence of the Spanish in the Americas or the dominance of the British and French in our Indigenous Pacific, we as First Peoples remain determined to be free of injustice. We will work with anyone black or white for our liberation. We will not rest until the cause of love and goodness overcomes bigotry and hate. As we plan for freedom and after, not even the most brutal force can deny our humanness or the love we have for peace, our peoples and our land. Change will come. Change is upon us.

The Earth is now more vulnerable to global warming and climate change than at any time in our history. Contamination of air, soil, water and land requires a greater global response in human coexistence and cooperation. Through practices of harmony and balance, we the First Peoples have always known the difference between good and bad development and that nature and humankind are inextricably linked. The world's more than 250 million Indigenous peoples have engaged in sustainable eco-friendly practices that hold the key to the very existence of our earth and the human species. Partnerships with Indigenous peoples are crucial to the future – in particular the environmental conservation and restoration of the planet's eco-systems. Indigenous peoples and knowledges are important collaborators with governments as we move to a more sustainable future. The contributing poets to this anthology are an exciting new generation of young Mapuche writers, largely university educated, who are politically active, highly organised and writing for freedom. The poetry and translation itself provides an excellent illustration of the determination of colonised communities to maintain their cultural and linguistic identity through the sharing of resistance stories.

The most important feature of the anthology is that all contributors raise some extremely far reaching questions about Mapuche injustice, death, life, love, compassion, struggle and reconciliation – to a wider global audience. In this sense Mapuche writers' invisibility in the Pacific and elsewhere has been overcome. This is a refreshing change from the past where texts in Australia included Mapuche as: subjects without voice; distorted interpretations of Indigenous experiences; and western deficit views masqueraded as reasoned argument. The eloquence of the text succeeds in throwing light on Mapuche dreams and aspirations by Mapuche themselves. While the poetry speaks to how injustice pervades Mapuche wellbeing, it also reveals, through sophisticated nuances, those warm and beautiful cultural spaces where colonialism does not penetrate. These spaces can be seen in Maribel Mora Curriao's Poem titled 'Dusk on the River' where a White Heron defies the afternoon. Similarly, Paulo Huirimilla's poem 'Navigator of the Blue Waterfall' is rich in echoes of the ancestors and marinated in Indigenous knowledges. These examples and many others reveal the sophistication of the new Indigenous political and intellectual agenda evident in the writings of first peoples worldwide. To achieve political sovereignty, we need to interrogate colonialism and non-Indigenous writings about us. However, to achieve what Native American scholar Robert Warrior calls Indigenous intellectual sovereignty, we must utilise and preserve to the fullest extent possible all that makes us unique and distinct as Indigenous peoples. While political sovereignty is a story about colonialism, Indigenous intellectual sovereignty is stories by, for and about ourselves. Books like this anthology are rare. Equally rare is fine poetry by a talented new generation of young Mapuche writers. Immerse yourself in their words then pass this profoundly important book on to all to read.

– Professor Lester-Irabinna Rigney PhD
Dean, Indigenous Education, University of Adelaide, Australia

The Mapuche Nation and its Poetry

– Jaime Luis Huenún Villa

The Mapuche population in Chile comprises, according to official figures, 604,349 people, making up 4% of the total population of the country. However, other demographic statistics provided by Indigenous organisations and academic institutions indicate that 1,500,000 individuals identify as members of this first nation.

It is important to note that 60.7% of the Mapuche population live in the cities of Puerto Montt, Osorno, Valdivia, Temuco, Concepción, Valparaíso and of course, Santiago, the populous capital city. These "urban Mapuches", as they have been known for some time, reside in marginal and peripheral sectors and are employed mostly as workers in industry, commerce and domestic services.

On the other hand, 39.3% of our population still live in regional zones in the interior in the communes or settlements (Indigenous reserves), maintaining a subsistence economy based on agriculture and livestock directed toward self-autonomy, and work linked to the sporadic manufacturing of ancestral crafts (textiles, pottery, silver ornaments, carving of native wood, among other types of craftsmanship).

The Mapuche language, named Mapudungun (the language of the Earth) or Mapuchedungún (the language of the people of the Earth) is, according to UNESCO, listed among the endangered languages destined to disappear.

According to exploratory studies published in 2007 by the Chilean linguist, Fernando Zúñiga, only 143,862 Mapuches would have a grade of active competence in their mother tongue, and 262,935 community members would have a passive competence, which is to say, they do not speak the language but do understand conversations in Mapudungun.

In light of these statistics, the national Mapuche language is in a critical phase, its current status a reflection of the historical challenges that the people of the earth have had to face to ensure that their traditions and cultural principles prevail.

And so it is this first nation, the only one that could stop the advance of the Spanish Conquest in South America (a heroic achievement that inspired the prestigious epic poem *La Araucana* by Alsonso de Ercilla), has received until the present a difficult and asymmetric treatment by the national Chilean state, which in 200 years of republic has incurred grave losses – human, cultural and territorial. During the war named the Araucanian Pacification (1881–1883), Chile routed the Mapuche armies and effectively annexed the Araucanian region to the administration and control of the government.

Thus, what was the Mapuche Nation, whose natural borders until the middle of the nineteenth century were the Bío-Bío river in the north, and the Toltén river in the south (from the 36° parallel to 39–37° South), was left in the hands of Fisco (the state), the colonisers, the adventurers and speculators of lands. The Mapuches who survived the Pacification were given rugged terrain with difficult access, and were subject from this time to a politics of assimilation that utilised "pacifying" strategies (education, evangelisation and an unequal integration into the economic system) and the more violent (persecution, assassination, usurpations, burning of houses and crops, incarceration, etc.).

During the course of the twentieth century, part of the Mapuche society organised and educated itself and elaborated diverse strategies to defend its cultural patrimony, world view and the remnants of territory assigned to them by the state. In this long process of searching out political spaces to obtain autonomy and self-determination, the Mapuche people have also generated artistic movements that, to a greater or lesser extent, have echoed the issues of their time as much as the conservation and dynamic projection of aspects of their own culture.

In this context, Mapuche poetry constitutes one of the most relevant literary phenomena to arise in Chile in the past two decades. Since 1988 to date, a score of Mapuche authors have been regularly publishing books, thereby establishing a distinctive and diverse lyrical poetics. We are talking about a poetic output that has attenuated in part the Eurocentric literary culture present throughout the twentieth century in a country that was only capable of valuing and honouring works with a strong affiliation with Greco-Roman, European and Anglo-Saxon aesthetics.

Authors such as Leonel Lienlaf, Lorenzo Aillapán, José Teiguel, Bernardo Colipán, María Isabel Lara Millapán, Elicura Chihualilaf, María Teresa Panchillo, Marcial Colín, Juan Paulo Huirimilla, Maribel Mora Curriao, César Millahueique, among many others, have created in their works a territory that preserves and projects community and family histories, the shameful tragedies and denials suffered by their people, and the collective symbols of a human group that fights daily to give continuity to their culture in a space that, as we have discussed, is often-times restrictive and adverse.

Mapuche literature is not only founded on the old songs but also the contemporary trends and poetics in Chile and Latin America. In this regard, we can say that Mapuche poetry remains in a voluntary suspension and tension between the archaic and the modern, resisting being constituted only in signifiers, its principal characteristic being to establish, realise and develop permanent and lived connections with family and community memory and the traditional, aesthetic oral discourses.

We present to the dear Australian reader a small offering of this growing lyrical production, inspired by a desire to share a handful of poems in which the powers of the landscape and the word are combined with strong and deeply rooted mythical beings and painful, current political conflicts; poems in which the ceremonial use of two languages (Mapudungun and Spanish) testify to the visionary works of the poetry inside a society that has managed to maintain alive a luminous and at the same time a complex collective memory, a memory that, in definition, nourishes and revitalises the songs and acts of a nation that refuses to disappear.

El arte de la palabra/The art of the word

One of the more abhorrent crimes of Christianity and Western civilisation consists in convincing the masses that words are only signifiers. – Roque Dalton[1]

Democracy is a work of art. It is not a fixed state. It is something that is constructed in the day by day coexistence and at the same time is an opposition and negation of the state, because it breaks up with hierarchic systems. It is based in mutual respect. – Humberto Maturana[2]

Poetry is not isolated from the world. It does not belong to a specialist domain. Poetry is a reflexive exercise, not just entertainment. Poetry allows us to follow the flux of our embodied thoughts; embodied because without our bodies we do not exist. Hence poetry is reflexion. Keeping this in mind, the poetry in this anthology allows readers to acknowledge and reflect upon the values that are important in the construction of a global world with its emphasis on a utopian neo-liberal economy. If you are patient with me I would like to introduce this anthology in two parts: an extended first section, in which I shall explore the relationship between European Modernity and its periphery; and a second section, in which I will make some points about the Mapuche nation and their art of the word.

The consequences of European Modernity in its periphery.

Mapuche people are people exiled in their own territory. Any engagement with Indigenous nations of the planet needs to deal with the fact that Western civilisation has reduced their power, epistemologies, identities and cultural practices to something

---

[1] Roque Dalton, *Poesia*. San Salvador: Editorial Universitaria, s/f, p.180. My translation.

[2] Humberto Maturana R., *La democracia es una obra de arte*. Colombia: Cooperativa Editorial Magisterio, no publication date. My translation.

backward and in need of purging. On the other hand, the Western world privileges rationality and its scientific and technological advancements. This anthology celebrates the extent to which poetry has always been firmly engaged with the flux of orality[3] – an art that the West has captured in the written word as an art of the book. The poetry of the world of the South, based on the *ül*[4], gives testimony to the struggle of the Mapuche people against forgetting their heritage, and brings forth their voices, cultural complexities and sometimes contradictions. Paulo Huirimilla evokes this clearly in 'Warrior Song', where the poet says that his is a 'stuttering' voice.

The Chilean state occupation of Mapuche territory continues up until this day through the expansion of neo-liberal economic practices into Mapuche communities. New territories are required to satisfy the ever-growing need for resources to sustain this blind economic ideology, which gives rise to a selfish and ultimately self-destructive community. Humans are consuming their future in the worst plague that the planet has seen[5]. The sense of loss this long process of colonisation produces in Mapuche subjectivities is clear in many of the poems by Roxana Miranda Rupailaf, Paulo Huirimilla and Maribel Mora Curriao. In particular, Curriao's poems 'Our Songs Remained Behind' and 'Dreams in the Valley' convey the poet's struggle to communicate with her ancestral past, having lost her Mapudungun language. The loss of language breaks the bond with the Earth, the stories that web that bond and her Mapuche

[3] See Walter J. Ong, *Orality and Literacy. The Technologizing of the Word*. London: Methuen & Co., 1982.

[4] The *ül* is the song and poetry and it is part of the *Mapuche* art of the word involving subgenres relating to the use of it in many cultural practices such as those related to healing, *rogativas*/praying, warrior songs and others.

[5] Flannery, Timothy, *The Future Eaters. An Ecological History of Australia*. Port Melbourne: Reed Press 1994. The important question here is related to the velocity the development of technologies brought forth by the present detached way of seeing our place in the biosphere is producing changes in the capacity living systems have to reproduce themselves. The actual consuming velocity is increasing in such a way that in all areas of our lives we are exhausting and destroying the living systems that allow us to exist. In other words, we are structurally de-coupling in relation to our natural niches and environments, risking the biosphere's life.

lineage. Hers is a gaze that wants to recover its origins – a nostalgic gaze toward the ancestral valleys. When I say ancestral I do not imply long past, but passing now ancestral, because its epistemology, which has lasted for millenia without destroying the environment, is today being confronted with the destructive intrusion into Mapuche communities of the neo-liberal mindset.

Mapuche cultural practices and ways of living continue to be dismantled and assimilated into a homogeneous nation state. Pinochet's dictatorship in Chile experimented with and adapted the neo-liberal ideology before exporting it back to the United States and England, where it originated. In the process, the Mapuche people have been reduced to second-class citizens and dependant clients of a state in the continual throes of privatisation. Chile is a state that conceives itself as a mediator in the two-fold process of expanding and privatising itself: the state as war machine in a never-ending process of re-territorialisation. Vernacular modes of living are destroyed to pave the way for modernity – the institutions, companies and subjectivities that are seen as integral to the colonial project. Mapuche people are reduced to the condition of clients and competitors in a world in which everything is up for sale. It is in the context of war against nature and its custodians – the Indigenous populations of Chile – that the poetry in this anthology comes forth and opens up for *winka*/foreigner readers new domains of existence to observe, reflect and learn from,[6] so we can open our eyes and

---

[6] In general in Latin America "intercultural" educational programmes are seen and promoted as the key to overcome the present isolation of Indigenous cultures. In Chile there are some programmes that pursue intercultural objectives, but are always seen as from the perspective of the white populations, i.e., the Mapuche are to become intercultural to survive. The point must be that the general Chilean society learn/live about the Mapuche ways so as to be able to critically question the inertia of the general status quo and be able to survive the destruction brought forth by neo-liberal economic policies. This is not an idealism, but a profound form of realism as Humberto Maturana has clearly stated in an interview in which he says that the Mapuche "considered themselves part of the dynamic of nature. Mapuches and Pehuenches considered themselves as part of the world", concluding that "I do not think that Indigenous people are particularly virtuous but they had a different view of the natural world, a view that is negated by us because we do not have it. We are

demand that democracy be democratised.

Mapudungun: the Language of the Earth.

The neo-liberal economic expansion into Mapuche communities ruptures the connection human beings have with the Earth. What we have instead is a floating national identity, sustained by the destruction of Indigenous populations, characteristic of colonial nation-states around the world. A soldier mentality is at play in an imaginary domain where there are no roots or firm ground to stand upon. All that remains is a permanent state of war for new markets, territories, clients, resources and citizens. These floating mythologies of national identity (which this migrant 'I' knows only too well) are sustained by the violence of the grand narratives of progress and capitalism. The colonial project is dressed up as the civilisation and democratisation of primitive society, a linear evolution from barbarianism to enlightenment and the spoils of modernity. However, the freedom that the West speaks of is not practised in those countries that are situated within the borders of modernity/coloniality[7]. While the Western concept of parliamentary democracy is privileged, other forms of democracy are suppressed. The relationship with the Earth becomes the focus of the violence of the dark side of the colonial dream. And so it is that Indigenous populations today are suffering a low intensity 4th World War[8].

---

not people of the Earth. We belong to a culture that has separated human beings from the world and has placed the natural world, the animal world, and the vegetal world at its service. We are the kings of nature, and to be kings implies being blind about our servants." In Marcelo Mendoza's *Todos queríamos ser verdes. Chile en la crisis ambiental.* Santiago: Planeta, 1994, pp. 49-50. My translation.

[7] Modernity/coloniality is a concept created by Walter Mignolo to explain the double sided shaping of European Modernity in the Americas. See his *Local Histories/Global Designs. Coloniality, Subaltern Knowledges, and Border Thinking.* Princeton, New Jersey: Princeton University Press, 2000. Also see Aníbal Quijano, "Coloniality of Power, Eurocentrism, and Latin America", *Neplanta: Views from the South* 1.3, 2000, Duke University Press: 533-580.

[8] Subcomandante Marcos, *Our Word is Our Weapon. Selected Writings.* London: Serpent's Tail, 2001.

Chile is celebrating two hundred years since its independence from Spain. One must ask, what is being celebrated? What kind of country is being brought forth? What sort of a nation is imagined? Is there a dialogue between cultures[9] toward a common view of the world we all want to live in, of citizenship and our place in it? How are different views about the relationship with the Earth, self, and community seen and allowed legitimate existence? Has there been any questioning of the current liberal idea of the state? What do we have to say about the state that has ruled up until now? Has it been comprehensive? Need it be changed? Does it have the plasticity to allow all cultural differences to be part of it? Does it have something to learn from other cultural and Indigenous experiences? All of these questions are intimately related to the value we give to the spoken word.

AdMapu/El rostro de la tierra/The face of the Earth.

The Mapuche poets in this anthology produce a voice that allows us, readers/listeners, to bring forth a more coherent and balanced conception of the word. The word is not out there but comes into existence through our word-actions. We bring the world into being when we speak it and live it. The word in the Mapuche world reveals a totally different view of the role human societies play in relation to their place on the Earth. Mapuche culture is centred in the word[10]. Language has a strong social value in Mapuche culture: Mapudungun, the language of the Earth. The use and value of the word has a powerful communal sense. The very name of the community shows the vinculum between the Earth and its people: Mapuche, people (*che*) of the Earth (*Mapu*). Elicura Chihuailaf

[9] At present, after some intents by previous post-dictatorship governments to solve the problems that impede the relation, the Chilean state has, under the pressure of the Chilean right, applied the Antiterrorist Laws, written down and established during Pinochet years, to the Mapuche populations fighting for their lands. This criminalisation undoes all possibilities to establish any meaningful conversation and it is in this sense that I speak of a low intensity war between that State and the Mapuche people.

[10] Lucía Golluscio, *El pueblo Mapuche. Poéticas de pertenencia y devenir.* Buenos Aires: Editorial Biblos, 2006.

teaches us that Mapuche culture is sustained by the *Itro Fil Mogen*, a totality without exclusion in which all living beings, *lo viviente*, take part. And because time is circular, Mapuche people leave tracks, in their walking through life, that reach the past as well as the future[11].

Leonel Lienlaf[12], a Mapuche poet whose work is not in this anthology, says that 'when you are a habitant of a space, you live that hill because the hill allows you to do so and you embrace that hill as your own.' In other words, in interacting, the hill and you bring forth a common history, which is the product of the structural coupling[13] taking place between them. Lienlaf explains:

> everything is interrelated. The community is not only the people that live the territory and place but also the sacred elements, the cosmic, the ancestors. This is the reason you cannot make a community anywhere, because the communities are built in ancestral places.

This structural coupling between humans and nature brings into question the conceptualisation of self as something encapsulated and closed off from everything else; a self that does not take responsibility for the consequences of its own actions. Isn't this what we hear from the most recalcitrant right wing ideology? That our behaviour is not responsible for the destruction of the environment? That it is nature which destroys itself? We can see now the threat Mapuche and all other Indigenous nations in the world today pose to the expansion of Capitalism. Hence the current application by the Chilean Government of antiterrorist laws, created by Pinochet, to the Mapuche people.

The Earth has a power, force and energy in the poems in this

---

[11] Elicura Chihuailaf, "Introducción. En el azul de la palabra", in Sebastián Quepul Quintremil, José Santos Lincomán Inaicheo, Anselmo Raguileo Lincopil, *Poesía Mapuche. Las raíces azules de los antepasados*. Temuco: Universidad de la Frontera, 2003, p. 16.

[12] Patricia Junge (1999), "Leonel Lienlaf: los Mapuches somos el pueblo que más dialoga", *Plaza pública. Revista de política y ciudadanía*, No 8, Octubre-noviembre 1999.

[13] Structural coupling is a concept that describes the interdependence between living systems. See Humberto Maturana Ro. & Gerda Verden-Zoller, *The Origins of Humanness in the Biology of Love*. UK: Imprint-Academic, 2008.

anthology that does not exist in narrow and detached Western views of the world. In the Mapuche world the powerful bond between people and place takes the shape of three main forms of cultural knowledge, transmitted from generation to generation through stories and conversations around the fire, *el fogón*, in the *ruka/* house. The three forms are: the *Geh*; *perrimontun*; and *pewma*. An overview of each of these fundamental concepts in Mapuche culture is provided below.

Firstly, the *Geh* are immaterial beings who are the custodians of the different places shaping the Mapuche territory. It is in this sense that the Earth, the Mapu, is sacred, full of life energy and populated by immaterial beings that we must respect as they are the custodians of the rivers, hills, mountains and all places. In other words, the Mapuche people are not alone, but are structurally coupled to the Earth and its places. In 'A Child in the Path of his Dream', by Omar Huenuqueo Huaiquinao, this sacred, respectful dimension of life is realised in the figure of a child who converses with the world around him. The child lives in a world where he is not alone, where there is no solitude because everything is meaningful and alive. The poem demonstrates the important role conversation plays in maintaining the balance between the dualities that form this world. In the Western world, where nothing is sacred, this side of life becomes a horror movie, a dangerous, feared and dark side that must be conquered or destroyed, or rapidly dismissed as backward. All of the poets included in this anthology give testimony to this structural coupling, for example, in María Isabel Lara Millaipán's poem 'Mangin', where 'the rain says what I think'. But this sacred balance or vinculum is at risk, as is the case in the beautifully dark poem 'Rauquemo Piwkan/Cisnes de Rauquemó/Rauquemó Swans', by Jaime Huenún, bringing forth a non-idealistic Mapuche world. Places have a sacred dimension because *Geh* have a tutelary function; they protect the Mapu.

Secondly, these spirits communicate with the living through *perrimontun*, which are apparitions of beings in real life (animals, especially birds and snakes) that have a supernatural quality that allows them to cross natural frontiers or become invisible/visible. Their apparition announces something which may affect individuals or the community, therefore the *perrimontun* needs to be carefully interpreted. This presence emerges in full in Omar Huenuqueo Huaiquinao's poems in which poetry is a mirror of nature bringing forth happiness and life so every living system (animals, especially birds – the turtledove and thrush), objects (a chair), and atmospheric phenomena (a breeze) are expressive of the continuity of the dance of life. Two poems by Maribel Mora Curriao, the first, 'Song for my Mother', testifies to the above when she says that '*Perrimontun*/ is nothing more than that/ a brief sojourn/ in the sky' and, the second, '*Perrimontun*', which refers to the supernatural experiences a Machi/ shaman receives when being initiated by her mother.

Thirdly, these apparitions manifest themselves through *pewma*/ dreams in which deceased family members are dreamed as having a normal life, in dialogue or giving up a message that is pertinent to the dreamer or his/her community. The knowledge of deceased family members is brought to life in these conversations, where dead and living members of the family come together conversing in a natural way. The separation between the dead and the living is, in *pewma*, overcome so that ancestral knowledge is passed down through the generations. Mapuche culture is thus maintained and passed through circular time into new generations. The emphasis is on the connection between ancestry and new generations instead of the lineal separation lived in the West. Such is the creativity and plasticity of Mapuche ways of thinking and doing, capable of solving a problem Western thought is unable to confront in an affirmative way. The Mapu/Earth is a shared space, *espacio compartido*, full of force and power. In Mapuche culture there is no construction of temples because the Mapu/Earth itself is the temple. This is the case in María Isabel Lara Millaipán's poem 'Relmu', where the present is open to the past because the memory of the past is inscribed in place. But this shared space can be broken as is clear in Maribel Mora Curriao's poem 'Dreams in the Valley'.

Sin miedo/Without fear.

Mapuche poetry is not simply entertainment, it cannot be, but is
an epistemic tool in which a language domain is open so that these
Mapuche poets observe themselves and reflect about the actual
configuration of their self and its relation to the world they are
structurally coupled to. Mapuche poetry expands consciousness
and enlarges the reflective space Mapuche poets need to explore
the relationship between self and other (Mapuche and Chilean),
between self and the world (the Chilean state, the Mapuche
traditions), between self and nature (the Earth). The poems are rich
in cultural references, and sometimes travel from as far as Mexico,
through popular music, as is the case of Paulo Huirimilla's uses
of *'el corrido'*. Huenún makes intertextual references to German
and Chinese poetry, and Maribel Mora Curriao quotes T.S. Eliot.
Mapuche poetry is a domain open in writing in which the poet
explores their own complexities and contradictions, product of
their double, happy and painful, intercultural status, as well as
the contradicting behaviours and desires coming out of this fact.
But this expansion of consciousness applies also to *winka* readers,
because it touches the inner-most self, one that is beyond neo-liberal
ideologies, in which our deepest desire, to live a life in balance with
the earth, emerges strongly. This is why poetry is not simply another
commodity, to use and discard, for the neo-liberal world market,
but a more profound epistemic dispositive which allows Mapuche,
Chileans and all *winka* readers to engage in a way of living that is as
complex as well as problematic as any other when true to itself.

I hope, as a winka reader, that all readers of this anthology are
willing to open themselves up and learn the art of conversation
which these poems invite. It is in this way that the first epigraph
to this introduction should be understood. Words are not only
signifiers, floating signifiers as Jacques Derrida would have us believe,
but also they are the tools and the body itself that they carve and, as
such, they are Mapuche embodied experiences. The second epigraph
reminds us that democracy is not just a representative parliamentary
voting system, but a long and empowering art of conversation, or
art of the word, inclusive of those whom our certainties blind us to

see. This inclusiveness is nothing less than what we call listening, something which is scarcely practised in world politics. Democracy is brought to hand as part of the art of listening. If you accept that the above arguments make sense, then I can say that they are the flesh of the conversations they make possible. This is the reason why speaking is an art, an ancient art, which implies the need to listen to those who have been able to master this art if we want to produce a truly coherent and democratic global society. Theirs is the true word. Do we want to take up this opportunity and begin, leaving behind our certainties, to open up ourselves and listen to the conversation we are allowing ourselves to participate in?

– Dr. Sergio Holas Véliz
The University of Adelaide

Poetry of the Earth:
Trilingual Mapuche Anthology

BERNARDO COLIPÁN

KAWELLU MU ÜTRÜNARÜN WÜMAW MU CHUMÜL PUN

Fütrake milla longko mülepuy wenu mapu.
Fey itro alü tripa, müli ñi shillan kawell.
Epuchi lukutun fey tañi weñangkün mu ka ñi llükan
    ngüman.
Inayawülenew püllomeñ.

Pürakintufiñ wenu chew tañi ngünemapulepumum ñi
    milla püylawe
Kizu ñi kallfü malen engü fey rakinagümfin ñi pu
    pewma.

DEL CABALLO CAÍ AL SUELO LA OTRA NOCHE

Cabezas grandes de oro están en el cielo.
Y ya lejos de mí está mi cabalgadura.
Me arrodillo dos veces y lloro de angustia y miedo.
La muerte me persigue.
Miro hacia arriba donde reina mi cuchillo de oro
con su reina azul y cuento mis sueños.

I FELL FROM MY HORSE THE OTHER NIGHT

Giant heads of gold are in the sky.
And now, far from me, my horse.
I kneel twice and cry with anguish and fear.
Death follows me.
I look to the sky where my gold knife reigns
with its blue queen and I tell my dreams.

PULOTRE 1916

Mufüngechi rikewfuy lan
Kürüf mew fey may kizu ñi changül kuwü mu wirikay
Kiñe ange iñche ñi ange ürkenonga.
Akun kintugafiel chi chülkü
Lapakonkülelu latuwe ñi tapül mew.
Feymu pizümkawi kom fichi trokiñ che.
Ella ayekafuyngün, welu müli nga yewün
Ütrünarkünerpulu ñi pu kalul engün. Fey kake
impolngeyngün nga
Ñi pontro mew.
Iñche kay we rakinen mari kechu tripantü
Pefilu nga mongen iñche lemawün kiñe trewa reke
Ütrüftükungelu trufken mew.
Femlu fey eypifin may nga ñi peñi:
Pengelelayu chemngen ta llükan kiñe
Runa trufür mew. (Eliot)
Tüngkülekallenge.
Lan ta kiñe weza züngu ka müten, kake züngu türpu
  pifal-lay.

PULOTRE[1] 1916

Varias veces la muerte intentó cuajarse
en el aire y con su dedo dibujó el perfil
de un rostro que no era el mío.
Llegó buscando la señal
tatuada en las hojas del latúe[2].
Ahí se desarmó toda esa familia.
Trataron de sonreír, pero algo en sus cuerpos
se desprendía. Y luego los envolvieron
a cada uno en sus frazadas.
Y yo sólo contaba quince años
cuando vi a la vida huir como un perro
arrojado a las cenizas.
Entonces le dije a mi hermano:
Te mostraré lo que es el miedo en un
                    puñado de polvo. (Eliot)
Permanece tranquilo.
La muerte es un accidente, lo demás no tiene
   importancia.

---

[1] Los relatos orales huilliches cuentan que en 1916, en la localidad de Pulotre, sector de la cordillera de la Costa de Osorno, una pareja de ancianos fue quemada viva por estar contagiada de viruela, enfermedad que causaba gran mortandad en la época. El poema se basa en ese hecho registrado por la memoria de los indígenas más ancianos.

[2] Arbusto espinoso de gran poder alucinógeno que crece en el sur de Chile. Su fruto es muy venenoso. Posee un poderoso alcaloide que produce demencia a quien lo ingiere. Los chamanes mapuches lo usaban de manera muy dosificada en ciertas ceremonias para producir alucinaciones.

PULOTRE[3] 1916

Many times death tried to set
in the air and with a finger drew the profile
of a face that was not mine.
It came looking for the sign
tattooed on the leaves of the latúe[4].
There it undid that entire family.
They tried to smile, but something in their bodies
became detached. And afterwards they wrapped
each one of them in their blankets.
And I was only fifteen
when I saw life run like a dog
thrown on the ashes.
So I told my brother:
I will show you fear
                            in a handful of dust. (Eliot)
Stay calm.
Death is an accident, nothing else matters.

---

[3] Huilliche oral histories tell that in 1916, in the locality of Pulotre, an area of the cordillera in the Costa de Osorno, an old couple was burnt alive for contracting smallpox, a disease that caused great loss of life in that epoch. The poem is based on this fact recorded in the memory of the oldest Indigenous people.

[4] A spiny bush and strong hallucinogen that grows in the south of Chile. The fruit is very poisonous and has a powerful alkaloid that induces madness in those who ingest it. Mapuche shamans used controlled dosages of the plant in certain ceremonies to invoke hallucinations.

SECHUAN REKE KONÜN-NGELAY PANGIMAPU RÜPÜ

Li Po ta epe püñeññengelu
Ñi ñuke pewmarki ñi anünarpan Venus mapu ñi mollo mew
Feymu lle Li Po üytuntukufi,
Llüfezüfe pilerkey fachi üy tati.
Sechuan,
Üyechi mapu chew müñawkefumum chi ülzüngufe,
Wingkulkawküli ka mawüzantükawküli
Pepi konün-ngenolu
Tüfaw Pangimapu reke chew rumel
Wüñokel ta che fichi kamapu ngewüyetuchi peñi reke
Yepapetulu tami inangüman pünon tati.
Kizulelu kay eymi mangelfimi
Tami llawfeñ engü küyen pütual
Üyechi inangüman kolka.
Welu küyen kimlafi pülku, tami llawfeñ kay
Re inayentumekeymu müten.
Pu zumiñ re kiñe tritrang nge müten küze reke peyefali.
Kiñe antü
Kake mapu tuwlu kellukünueyew.
Konümpa ta wirikamekefi üyechi zomo
Ñi ange poyekefulu eymi tichi püramüwün mew nga
Rupalu ta kiñe warangka aylla pataka meli mari tripantü
Mu fey mulfen kay
La ngollilen nüwküli pu anümka ñi tapül mew.

11

DIFÍCIL COMO EL DE SECHUÁN ES EL CAMINO A PANGUIMAPU[5]

Poco antes de nacer Li Po
su madre soñó que en su seno caía el planeta Venus
y por eso le dio el nombre
de Po, que significa "el luminoso".
Sechuán,
la tierra en que anduvo el poeta,
está llena de cerros y montañas
de difícil acceso
como aquí en Panguimapu donde siempre
vuelves como el hermano muerto
a recoger tus últimas pisadas.
Como estás solo invitas a beber
a tu sombra y a la luna
el último trago.
Mas la luna no sabe de bebidas y tu sombra
se limita a imitarte.
Un ojo desnudo en la noche es la única luz imaginable.
Un sol
de otra parte les tiende la mano.
La memoria dibuja el rostro
de la mujer que amaste en la cosecha
de mil novecientos cuarenta y el rocío
se sostiene
borracho entre las hojas de los árboles.

---

[5] Topónimo del mapudungun que significa "tierra del puma".
Localidad ubicada en San Juan de la Costa, provincia de Osorno,
décima región de Chile.

THE ROAD TO PANGUIMAPU[6] IS AS DIFFICULT AS THE WAY TO SZECHUAN

Not long before the birth of Li Po
his mother dreamt that the planet Venus fell in her womb
and that's why she gave him the name of Po
which means "the luminous one".
Szechuan,
the land where the poet walked
is full of mountains and hills
difficult to access
like here in Panguimapu where
you always return
like the dead brother
to recover your final footsteps.
Being alone you invite your shadow
and the moon
to share the last drink.
Though the moon knows nothing
of drinks and your shadow limits itself
to imitating you.
A naked eye in the night is the only imaginable light.
A sun
from another place extends its hand.
Memory draws the face
of the woman you loved in the harvest
of nineteen-forty and the dew
holds itself
drunk among the leaves of trees.

---

[6] Mapudungun place-name that means "land of the puma". A locality in San Juan de la Costa, Osorno province, tenth region of Chile.

FEY KIÑE ANTÜ PU CHEWKE REKE PEWMAYIÑ...

Fey kiñe antü pu chewke reke pewmayiñ
Nüymayafiel ñi azngellüwkülechi az chi witrungko.
Wizkeñkülen rupalafiel pu troltro
Ñi kuyfike züngu.
Malal mew petu kiñeke nülkülewey
Pu inangüman kelü palaw fün.
Kimelngewüyi tañi pu foro mew küpalen ta mawün.
Pu kürew zañeyeyngün ñüküf ñi wellingke nge mew.
Rüfküley may iñ züngu taiñ trekayawal
Üyechi rüpü püle chewnorume amunulu.
Puwtual nga che ruka mu
Fey üngümküleputual
Ta kiñe zomo fürenen eypiatew iñchiñ
Entuchafkülelafiel ñi tükunel chi takun
Tañi inal trafpan tripantü trawün mew.

Y TAMBIÉN UN DÍA COMO LAS GARZAS SOÑAMOS...

Y también un día como las garzas soñamos
arrebatar la revelada imagen de un estero.
Pasar silbando el antiguo
lenguaje de los cardos.
Aún quedan en el cerco
trepadas las últimas mosquetas[7].
Ya se anuncia en mis huesos la llegada de las lluvias.
Los mirlos anidan en los ojos
vacíos del silencio.
Estamos ciertos que debemos andar
caminos que conduzcan a ningún lado.
Llegar a casa
y esperar
a que una mujer nos pida
desabrochar su vestido puesto
en su última fiesta de cumpleaños.

---

[7] *Rosa moschata.* Arbusto de ramas delgadas y espinosas de origen europeo. Aparece como maleza en terrenos degradados. Su fruto se utiliza para hacer mermeladas y en la industria cosmetológica como reconstituyente de la piel.

ONE DAY WE DREAM AS HERONS DO...

One day we dream as herons do
to take the image of a stream
and go whistling the ancient
language of thistles.
The last of the mosquetas[8]
flower on the fence.
I feel the arrival of rain in my bones.
Blackbirds nest in my eyes
empty with silence.
We are certain we must take the path
leading nowhere.
Arrive home
and wait
for a woman to ask us
to undo the dress
she wore for her last birthday.

---

[8] *Rosa moschate* (Musk Rose). A type of rose bush with slender,
thorny branches of European origin. It appears as a weed in degraded
lands. The fruit is used to make jams and by the cosmetic industry to
make restorative skin products.

KURÜÑAMKU MALON

– A Likán Amaru

Wüllü mapu püle akulelngeyiñ
Züngu ta mülen kiñe malon.
Pepikawküley taiñ pu ülmen, tremoleyngün
Ka trepeleyngün pu wünenkona.
Piku mapu püle yeayiñmew
Pu payne kawell.
Küpalewüyey may, puliwen, pu peñi.
Küme püllü may kom iñchiñ nielayiñmew
Fentren kulliñ.
Trepelyefe, fochüm, tami kona.
Wewlimi küpalaymi zomo tami kurengeal.
Feychi üwelen kay ellkayafiyiñ
Münche kura.
Tami piwke, fochüm,
Ayüwngechi rüngkükaway
Kiñe choyke reke.

17

MALÓN DE KURIÑAMKO[9]

– A Likán Amaru[10]

De las tierras del sur nos llegan
noticias de un malón.
Listos están nuestros üllmenes[11], sanos
y despiertos los capitanes.
A las tierras del norte nos llevarán
los caballos celestes.
Ya viene, pues, la mañana hermanos.
Para todos tendrá la suerte
muchos animales.
Despierta, hijo, a tus mocetones.
Si ganas traerás mujer para casarte.
La soledad la ocultaremos
debajo de las piedras.
Tu corazón, hijo, saltará
alegre
como un choike[12].

---

[9] Linaje mapuche. Apellido que significa "aguilucho negro".
[10] Nombre propio. La palabra *Likán* hace referencia a ciertas piedras negras y pulidas, consideradas preciosas y mágicas, que la *machi* utiliza en sus trabajos rituales. Amaru es un nombre Inca que significa "serpiente del sol" o "serpiente brillante".
[11] Hombres mapuches ricos y respetados, poderosos económicamente.
[12] *El ñandú americano.* El baile del *choike* es una danza mapuche donde los varones imitan a esta ave. Es una danza de fertilidad que se baila en los ceremoniales.

KURIÑAMKO[13] RAID

– For Likán Amaru[14]

From the lands of the south comes
news of the raid.
Our ullmenes[15] at the ready, the captains
healthy and alert.
Celestial horses will carry us
to the lands of the north.
Well, morning approaches, brothers.
Everyone will share in the good fortune
of many animals.
Awake, my son, to your brave young friends.
If you win you will bring back a bride.
We will hide our solitude
under the stones.
Your heart, my son, will beat
with joy
like a choike[16].

---

[13] Mapuche lineage. A name that means "black hawk".

[14] A Mapuche personal name. The word Likán refers to polished,
black stones, considered to be precious and magical, which the machi
(medicine man or woman) uses in his rituals. Amaru is an Inca name
that means "serpent of the sun" or "shining serpent".

[15] Mapuche men who are rich and respected, powerful economically.

[16] The dance of the choike is a Mapuche dance where the men imitate
the Rhea darwini, a large, flightless ostrich type of bird native to
South America. It is a fertility dance performed in ceremonies.

LIKAN AMARU TAÑI WEFÜN

Ngelay kiñe kürüf, fotüm, fentre alükechi müpü nielu
Ka itro nowüngelu norume tami müpüw reke,
                                        Likan.
Tami kiñen fün ngerpuy chi antü.

Tami wüne nemül mew
            Ngülaen pimi
            Welling püle küpan
            Eluen tami wirikan.

¿Chew mülekeymi am petu tami küpakenon?

¿Kam tami llawfeñ zoy kuyfi tuwüy eymi mew?

Eymi ka iñche epu folilngeyu
Wümawkülelu kiñe fütra kuyfi mawüzantü mew.

Iñche eymimu ta mülen
Feymu lle kintuyawüleyu kürüf mu.
Antü ñi lif mew
Rakümkonkülelu tami yompewe mew.

APARICIÓN DE LIKÁN AMARU[17]

No hay un viento, hijo, tan alado
ni tan orgulloso como tu vuelo

Likán.

El sol fue tu única semilla.

Tu primera palabra fue
    ábreme
    vengo del vacío
    dame tu escritura.

¿ Dónde estabas antes que vinieras ?

¿ Acaso es tu sombra anterior a ti ?

Tú y yo somos dos raíces
dormidas en un bosque milenario.

Yo estoy en ti.
Por eso te busco en el aire.
En la pureza
del sol atrapado en tu cristal.

---

[17] Linaje mapuche. Apellido que significa "aguilucho negro".

APPARITION OF LIKÁN AMARU[18]

No wind, my son, is as swift
or proud as your flight,

                                  Likán.

The sun was your only seed.

Your first words were

                open me
                I come from the void
                give me your writing.

Where were you before you came?

Perhaps your shadow precedes you?

You and I are two roots
asleep in a millennial forest.

I am inside you.
This is why I search for you in the air.
In the purity
of the sun caught in your crystal.

---

[18] Mapuche lineage. A name that means "black hawk".

KIÑE KALLFÜ WENU ÑI FURI PÜLE TRAYAYTÜKUPUAY ÑI RAKIZUAM

Mülerki nga wiyuzkülechi wüllngiñ mew
Kiñe rangiñtükuwkülelu chew ta tüfa tañi wüñoletumum
Ngeno kalül
Trayaytükupatual tañi wellingke zumell engü.
Kalku may ñi zuam
Pürokawküley fachi trükofün
Tañi troy epu kuwü mew.

Kiñe kallfü wenu ñi furi püle trayaytükupuay ñi rakizuam.

Kanillo ta kintuyawülmanew ñi neyen
Wümañlu tüyechi kiñekelewechi filu ñi pel mew.
Zumiñküli mawün ñi ülkantun.
Ka femngechi pukemküli tañi fochüm ñi leliwülün mu.
Fey türpu kimwetulafin tañi pu trewa ñi wawakün
Lef narkülepalu wingkul püle engün.

Tüfachi kutran iñche tañi kimnoel chi züngu püle tuwlu.

Zewma punwüyi ngati iñche kay nien
Kiñe ngeno llawfeñ kalül müten,
Kiñe chong komütuwe
Ka kiñe nemül
Rumel wellilen wüñokelu.

"Iñche ta lali fey küpale tañi am, peay ka üyechi pu küllegtuwe ka müten chew ta iñche ñi müñawkefumum ka fey kimfemtuay tañi ruka." – Juan Pérez Jolote

23

DETRÁS DE UN CIELO AZUL IRÁ A GOLPEAR MI PENSAMIENTO

Hubo entre todas las puertas
irremediablemente una
a la que vuelvo ahora
sin cuerpo
a golpear con mis zapatos vacíos.
Kalku[19] fue el culpable
del calambre que se anuda
en los nudillos de mis manos.

Detrás de un cielo azul irá a golpear mi pensamiento.

Canillo[20] busca mi aliento
amanecido en el cuello de las últimas culebras.
Oscuro es el canto de la lluvia.
Es también invierno en la mirada de mis hijos.
Y no reconozco el ladrido de mis perros
que bajan de los cerros.

Dolor de cosas que ignoro.

Anochece y sólo tengo
un cuerpo sin sombra,
un espejo apagado
y una palabra
que siempre regresa vacía.

> Cuando yo muera y venga mi ánima, encontrará los mismos
> senderos por donde anduve y reconocerá mi casa.
> – Juan Pérez Jolote

---

[19] Brujo mapuche.
[20] Ser mítico maligno que forma parte de las creencias huilliches
(hombres del sur).

MY THOUGHTS WILL KNOCK BEHIND A BLUE SKY

Of all the doors
there was one
to which I now return
irremediably
without body
to knock with empty shoes.
Kalku[21] was to blame
for the cramp knotted
in the knuckles of my hand.

My thoughts will knock behind a blue sky.

Canillo[22] searches for my breath
that has awoken in the necks of the last snakes.
The song of rain is dark.
It is also winter in my sons' gaze.
I do not recognise the bark of my dogs
as they descend the hills.

The pain of things I ignore.

Night falls and all I have
is a body without a shadow,
a dull mirror
and a word
that always returns empty.

When I die and my soul comes, it will find the same paths
I walked and recognise my house. – Juan Perez Jolote

---

[21] A Mapuche sorcerer.
[22] An evil mythical being that forms part of the beliefs of the Huilliches (men of the south).

WÜÑOMEN WÜMKE

Tañi pu kuñülyen konümpawetulayngün üyechi wüllngiñ
ñi üy
Chew entuazeluwmum engün
Mañkaznefiel entuazchefe ñi kawell.
Chuchi chiwüznelu ñi trekan rumel wüñolekey ñi
    trüngkay mew.
Welu tañi pu kuñülyen wüñowelayngün
Üyechi troy antü mongen mew
Kolü azentungelu tüfeychi 1950 tripantü mu,
Iñche reke tañi pepi
Epuchi müñetunon tüyechi kafelekachi komew kay.
¿Welu amkay chunte püranetufi
Taiñ tripamum em
Iñ piwke?
Chem taiñ rüf poyekel müten mülekey,
Kake züngu kay re poz müten tati.
Fey kiñe antü kizu engün reke
Ñangümayiñ taiñ rakiñ
Fachi chunten taiñ chiwüzkantuyawüluwel
Kimafiel tachi wüñoletuamchi rüpü.
Antü müten may eypiay taiñ troy
Mongen ngütram em
Tañi ka femngechi ñi amulekan chi.

ARCO DEL RETORNO

Mis parientes no recuerdan el nombre de la plaza
en donde se retrataron
junto al caballo del fotógrafo.
Quien camina en torno a sí mismo vuelve siempre a su
    propio giro.
Pero mis parientes ya no vuelven
al momento
retratado en sepia en 1950,
como yo no puedo
dos veces bañarme en las mismas aguas.
¿Pero a qué altura
de nuestro punto de partida
se encuentra nuestro corazón?
Sólo lo que amamos verdaderamente permanece,
el resto es escoria.
Y también como ellos un día
perderemos la cuenta
de las vueltas que dimos en torno
a nosotros mismos
para conocer el camino de regreso.
Sólo el tiempo dirá si el fundamento
de lo que fuimos
siguió siendo el mismo.

ARC OF RETURN

My parents do not remember the name of the plaza
where they had their portrait taken
next to the photographer's horse.
He who walks in circles always returns to his own ways.
But my parents no longer return
to the moment
captured in sepia in 1950,
as I cannot
bathe twice in the same waters.
But how far
from our point of departure
do we find our heart?
Only that which we love truly remains,
the rest are dregs.
And one day we too
will lose count
of the turns we made around ourselves
to find our way back.
Only time will tell if the essence
of what we were
remains the same.

MARIBEL MORA CURRIAO

LLAGKÜLEWEY PU ÜLKANTUN

Chemnórume chem pifalwelay fanten antü.
Lángollilewi ti pun tañi müllo mew,
Fülmánengel tañi rakizuam kintuyawüleymu
                                    ¡oh, püllomeñ!
Kake antü kompañ.

Ellkawmekeymi, llamngeñ,
Munulüwmekeymi, llamngeñ.
¿chumül amta pepi pengégaymi?
¿chumül amta kimélfalpatugaymi tami akutual,
                                    Tami wüñotual?

Üyemu lloftuleymi, würwántuneymafiel
Tañi pu fochüm ñi neyen.
Üyemu ellkáwküleymi ñuke, llamngeñ, wenüy,
Kamapu züngun katrüzuamkelu ka llellipuymakelu,
Üyechi lef perimontun mew,
Feychi kom pu elürpa fochüm mew
Üwe pewmáyawlu engün.

Eypien: ¿chew amta ellkaneymi tami llumzüngu?
¿Chemu am ñüküfnárwümetuymi tüfa petu ngütrümeyu
nga?
¿Chemu am üwümlaymi wenu tami kuwü mew?
¿Chemu am apümlafimi chi nemül?
Üye engün lefmáwtripalu tañi lawélongko mu
Ka üye engün kütrókaneymanetew ñi müllo.

31

Llágkülewey pu ülkantun,
Uyülünmayew wellíng,
Tráflelinewchi kintuwülün
Chi wüño küpatun engü chi witrárupan
Ñi külleg rüpü.

Mawüzantü zoy kiñe konümpa ngelay ka
Feychi Edén chumkáwnurume üwümelngenulu iñchiñ.

¡Eymi kimnieymi ka, llamngeñ!
¡Eymi ñüküfnarümneymi, llamngeñ!
Müléwelay may tüyechi llegün antü,
Mülérpuki llegün antü ngati
Áfnagyüm wüla Ngünechen ñi nengüm
Kallfü wenu mew.

ATRÁS QUEDARON LOS CANTOS

Nada tiene sentido a esta hora.
Ebria la noche en mi cerebro,
trastocada mi razón te busca

                    ¡oh, muerte!

Compañera nuestra de cada día.

Cómo te escondes, hermana,
cómo te disfrazas, hermana.
¿Cuándo darás la cara?
¿Cuándo avisarás tu llegada,

                    tu regreso?

Allí estás acechando, nublando
la respiración de mis hijos.
Allí te ocultas madre, hermana, amiga,
lejana voz que coarta y que persigna,
en un perrimontun[23] no deseado,
a toda una estirpe de hijos
huérfanos de sueños.

Dime: ¿dónde ocultas tus secretos?
¿Por qué callas ahora que te llamo?
¿Por qué no señalas el cielo con tus manos?
¿Por qué no eliminas las palabras?
Esas que huyen de mis sienes
y aquellas que retuercen mi cerebro.

---

[23] Concepto que hace alusión a visiones y experiencias sobrenaturales que le ocurren a la persona que debe iniciarse como *machi* (chamán mapuche).

Atrás quedaron los cantos,
el vértigo y el vacío,
la mirada fija en sí misma
las huellas del retorno
y del exilio.

El bosque no es más que un recuerdo
del Edén que nunca nos fue prometido.

¡Tú lo sabes, hermana!
¡Tú lo callas, hermana!
Ya no existe el origen
y sólo existe el origen
hasta que se acabe
el impulso
de Gnechen[24]
en el
infinito.

---

[24] Divinidad superior de los mapuches. El dueño de la tierra y de la
gente.

OUR SONGS REMAINED BEHIND

Nothing makes sense at this hour.
The intoxicated night in my brain,
crazed my reason seeks you

oh, death!

Companion of our every day.

How do you hide yourself, sister,
how do you disguise yourself, sister.
When will you reveal your face?
When will you announce your arrival

your return?

There you are stalking, clouding
the breath of my children.
There you hide mother, sister, friend
distant voice that restricts and blesses
an undesired perrimontun[25]
to a whole lineage of children
orphans of dreams.

Tell me: where do you hide your secrets?
Why do you stay silent now that I call you?
Why do you not point to the sky with your hands?
Why not do away with words?
These that escape from my temples
and those that wring my brain?

---

[25] A concept alluding to the visions and supernatural experiences of a person initiated as a *machi* (Mapuche shaman).

Our songs remained behind,
vertigo and the void,
the gaze fixed on itself
traces of return
and exile.

The forest is no more than a memory
of an Eden that was never promised to us.

You know it, sister!
You silence it, sister!
The origin no longer exists
and only the origin exists
until the impulse
of Gnechen[26]
ends
in
infinity.

---

[26] A divine being of the Mapuches. Master of the Earth and people.

ÜYECHI PÜLOM MEW TA PEWMAN

Tüfa may iñche, wichunefilu ñi pu la,
Ñamküyawlu Aguila ñi pülom püle,
Ngoyünetufilu pewen engü mawüzantü.

Pewma mu ta pekefin
Tañi choyütripaken mollfüñ ñi kazi püle
Fey koñitripayekey fillke muntufe üñüm tañi lawe
longko mew
Iynarümfemmatew tañi pu kuwü ka tañi kewün ta iñche.

Welu, ka wüño choyütripatuy ñi kuwü
Ka kiñe we kewün
Wüño iymangelu ta iñche
Fey müchay nga ka tremtukay em
Tüfa ke ñochingechi ellkayawültufin
Pu metawe mew.
Welu ka pengekay em
Pu metawe
Feymay ñi pu wükan pacherkünungi
Pülom mapu püle.

Femlu fey witrapüran ka kalüluwtun,
Fey wefi tüfachi ange ka müten, fachi kalül ka müten
Ka fachi weñangkawün piwke ka müten.

Püllomeñ züngu may
Yafentunelanew fachi troy antü,
Itro fentre alümapunefiel mawüzantü may ñi zuam.

Pu pewütufe muntufe üñüm norume
– waylüpüran meli witran mapu püle –
Fachi ngünam poyewkülen may ñi zuam
Wüño müñawputual lil püle.

Welu, tüfamu ta mülen, kalül engü wümaw
Fachi paytre wente tafü mew.

SUEÑOS EN EL VALLE

Heme aquí, apartada de mis muertos,
perdida en el Valle del Águila,
olvidada del pehuén[27] y la montaña.

En sueños he visto
que brota sangre en mi costado
y nacen aves rapaces de mis sienes
que devoran mis manos y mi lengua.

Mas, me nacen otras manos
y otra lengua
que son devoradas nuevamente
y luego nacen otras
que oculto cuidadosa
entre metawes[28].
Pero también son alcanzados
los metawes
y sus restos dispersados
por el valle.

Entonces me levanto y me rehago,
la misma cara, el mismo cuerpo
y el mismo corazón acongojado.

---

[27] *Araucaria araucana*. Árbol que crece en la zona cordillerana
andina del sur de Chile. De este árbol los pehuenches (mapuches
de las montañas) extraen el piñón, también llamado *ngülliu* por los
mapuches, un fruto que tiene un 85% de almidón, un alto porcentaje
de calcio y hierro y que es el principal alimento de los pehuenches.
[28] Vasijas de barro de diferentes formas.

No es la muerte
quien me espanta a esta hora,
sino la distancia con las montañas.

No son los rapaces centinelas
—aúllo a los cuatro vientos—
sino el inútil deseo
del retorno a las quebradas.

Mas, heme aquí, cuerpo y sueño
sobre este suelo baldío.

DREAMS IN THE VALLEY

So here I am, removed from my dead,
lost in Eagle Valley,
forgotten by the pehuén[29] and the mountain.

In dreams I have seen
blood spring from my side
and rapacious birds born from my temples
devour my hands and tongue.

I grow other hands
and another tongue
only to be devoured again,
soon more are born,
which I carefully hide
among the metawes[30].
But the metawes
are also reached
and their remains scattered
in the valley.

So I rise and re-make
this same face, this same body
this same anguished heart.

---

[29] *Araucaria araucana* (Monkey Puzzle Tree). A tree that grows in
the cordilleran Andean zone in the south of Chile. From this tree
the Pehuenches (Mapuches of the mountains) extract pine kernels,
also known as *ngülliu*, a fruit that consists of 85% starch and a high
percentage of calcium and iron, and is the principal dietary intake of
the Pehuenches.
[30] Different types of earthenware vessels.

It is not death
who scares me at this hour
but the distance from the mountains.

It is not the rapacious sentinels
– I howl to the four winds –
but the vain desire
to return to the mountain ravines.

So, here I am, in body and dream
on this wasteland.

TAÑI ÑUKE ÜLKANTULELAL

¿Chem amta kimfalnuchi folil
Püñeñeymew am, ñuke,
Chem newen wenu mapu mew am
Llegfi tami pu antü?
Kom püle fütrake ülkantun tripay,
Üñüm tramültramül mew,
Ligke rayen wingkul püle
Waw mapu püle, afnuachi reke
Mechan mapu wirikamekelu tami küpayalchi mongen.

Femlu fey mawüzantü mew
Zañeluwingün pu yarken,
Wenu mapu pewtufe
Ellkayawülkelu, pepi kimngenuel
Tüyechi pu kümeke poyen pewtun züngu.
Wüle wall mapu ngetugaymi,
Tüfa traf müpüwkünuwmuyiñ
Elumuyiñ tami wenu mapu pelün.
Chemnorume katrütunelayiñmew,
Pekan ütrünarwümelayayiñ tami pu lipang mew,
Wall lulul mapu may taiñ
Wangkülen ngütantu ngey.

Zoy wechun amugayiñ,
Zoy wechun.
Chaw Ngünechen
Üngümneyiñmew.
Feyti perimontun may
Zoy fachi züngu ngelay tati,
Kiñe püchü mülemületupun
Wenu mapu mew.

43

Ñuke, tüfa ta alümapunewiyu,
Tamu witrampüramiyu tayu ruka
¡fa may chi zullin pülom!
Tamu rupayayu pun
Chumngechi tayu kake antü tripaken
¡chunten mollfüñ am püntefkawküli, ñuke!
Mülepegay may chuchi llowpagatew.
¿chumngechi chi mongeleay pu tromü
– rantumekeyu –
Ürkülen rakümlimi tami pu nge?
¿chumngechi am ngülayay wenu mapu
Ngenole tami pu ül?
¿iñi am pewmatutuay taiñ pu antü?
Chemnorume mongelelay, ñuke
Mongelenolimi,
Tichi kelü rayen ngütrümmekeymew,
Tichi foye ñi lig rayen,
Kachumu müñawyechi llampüzkeñ
Pewütuyawün tramültramül püle.
Newen püllütunge, ñuke, newen püllütunge
Witrampüramnge tami epu kuwü Puel Mapu püle,
Pekan keltawmakinolmew llükan,
Wekun antü mu tüyechi lan
Chem züngu nurume ngünenelay.

CANTO A MI MADRE

¿Qué extrañas raíces
te engendraron, madre,
qué prodigio en el cielo
dio origen a tus días?
Todo fue grandes cantos,
aves en el horizonte,
flores blancas en los cerros
y en los valles, interminables
surcos escribiendo tu futuro.

Entonces en el bosque
habitaron las lechuzas[31],
agoreras del Wenu Mapu[32]
ocultando, indescifrables,
los amorosos designios.
Mañana serás del mundo,
ahora vuela con nosotros
danos tu impulso de cielo.
Nada nos detiene,
en tus brazos no caemos,
el universo es nuestro
colchón de estrellas.

---

[31] *Tyto Alba*. Aves nocturnas que habitan en campos y zonas urbanas de Arica a Tierra del Fuego. Se alimenta de mamíferos pequeños, aves e insectos.

[32] La Tierra de Arriba, lugar al que ascienden las almas de los mapuches fallecidos. Concepto que hace referencia al territorio donde habitan los antepasados y adonde llegarán los mapuches que no transgredan o alteren las leyes y el orden natural de las cosas. En este espacio espiritual los mapuches se transforman en halcones o cóndores del sol.

Más arriba iremos,
más arriba.
Chao Gnechén[33]
nos espera.
El perrimontun[34]
no es más que eso,
una breve estadía
en el cielo.

Madre, estamos lejos ahora,
hagamos aquí nuestras tiendas
¡Este es el valle elegido!
Aquí pasaremos la noche
como cada vez que partimos.
¡Cuánta sangre disgregada, madre!
Habrá quién vendrá a recibirnos.

¿Cómo vivirán las nubes
-te pregunto-
cuando agobiados
cierres tus ojos?
¿Cómo abrirá el cielo
sin tus cantos?
¿Quien soñará nuestros días?
Nada vive, madre
si no vives,
la flor roja te reclama,
la blanca flor del canelo,
mariposas en la hierba
oteando en el horizonte.

---

[33] Divinidad superior de los mapuches. El dueño de la tierra y de la gente.
[34] Concepto que hace alusión a visiones y experiencias sobrenaturales que le ocurren a la persona que debe iniciarse como *machi* (chamán mapuche).

Vuelve en ti, madre, vuelve en ti
alza tus dos manos hacia Oriente,
que no te encadenen temores,
fuera del tiempo la muerte
no tiene ningún sentido.

SONG FOR MY MOTHER

What strange roots
engendered you, mother,
what miracle in the sky
gave rise to your days?
All was epic songs
birds on the horizon
white flowers in the hills
and in the valleys, endless
furrows writing your future.

In that time
Owls[35] inhabited the forest
omens of Wenu Mapu[36]
hiding, indecipherable,
amorous designs.
Tomorrow you will be of the world
now fly with us,
give us your impulse of sky.
Nothing holds us,
in your arms we do not fall,
the universe is our
bed of stars.

---

[35] *Tyto alba* (Barn Owl). A nocturnal bird that inhabits the fields
and urban zones from Arica to Tierra del Fuego. It feeds on small
mammals, birds and insects.

[36] The "Land of Above", the place where Mapuche souls ascend after
death. A concept that refers to the land inhabited by the ancestors
and the final destination of those Mapuches who do not transgress
or alter the laws and the natural order of the universe. In this spiritual
space the Mapuches metamorphose into falcons or condors of the
sun.

Higher we will go,
higher.
Chao Gnechen[37]
awaits us.
Perrimontun[38]
is nothing more than that,
a brief sojourn
in the sky.

Mother, we are far now,
let us make our camp here
this is the chosen valley!
We will spend the night here
like every other time we leave.
How much blood dispersed, mother!
There will be someone who comes to welcome us.

How will the clouds live
– I ask you –
when exhausted
you close your eyes?
How will the sky open
without your songs?
Who will dream our days?
Nothing lives, Mother,
if you do not live,
the red flower calls for you
the white flower of the cinnamon tree,
butterflies in the grass
searching the horizon.
Come to, Mother, come to
raise your hands towards the East
do not be chained by fears
outside time
death has no meaning.

---

[37] A divine being of the Mapuches. Master of the Earth and people.
[38] A concept alluding to the visions and supernatural experiences of a person initiated as a *machi* (Mapuche shaman).

NARANTÜYMAN ḼEWFÜ MEW

Kiñe lig chewké
Azel azeltulmekefí narantü.
Tañi mütréng kalül
Zoyfi tramültramül.
Ti llagentu züchingkén
Ñochi ñochingey ñi lemawün lewfü püle.
Fütra neyüy mapu may
Mongelerpual.

ATARDECER EN EL RÍO

Una garza blanca
desafía la tarde.
Su figura inmóvil
desborda el horizonte.
El último rayo de luz
huye sigiloso por el río.
La tierra respira hondo
para seguir viviendo.

DUSK ON THE RIVER

A white heron
defies the afternoon.
Its motionless figure
spills over the horizon.
A last ray of sun
escapes stealthily down the river.
The earth breathes deeply
and lives on.

ḼINGAFNAG WECHUKEY YÓMPEWE ÑI WAYCHÜF PÜLE

Itro pütrü pürá trongé tapül püle
Lelíwülnenew kiñe üwe lloyká
Fey ta kutránzuamyewümenew.
¡ta iñché! Fentré rakümkawkülelu
Fachí melí trengkü ruka mew.

EL AMANECER OCURRE TRAS LOS CRISTALES

Desde lo alto del follaje
una loica[39] solitaria me mira
y me compadece.
¡A mí! tan protegida
en estas cuatro paredes.

---

[39] *Sturnella loyca*. Ave de llamativo pecho rojo que habita desde Atacama a Magallanes.

DAWN BEHIND THE WINDOWS

From the top of the foliage
a solitary loica[40] looks at me
and takes pity.
On me! so protected
by these four walls.

---

[40] *Sturnella loyca* (Long-tailed meadowlark). A bird with a pronounced
red chest found from Atacama to Magallanas.

SHUMSHÚMNAG MEW

Tüféychi küntró fücha triwkü
Lüyütukontupáy tañi azkintutripawe mew.
Ñüküfngechi azkíntunenew,
Katrüntükunefi kámapu zuam.
Ináfülmayawüleyew reké weñangkün
Üyechi ülkántukenochi üñüm.
Lüykükonküley áfmollfüñal
Chi kashü rimu wenu.

EN LA PENUMBRA

Un tiuque[41] viejo y cojo
se asoma a mi ventana.
Me mira con sigilo,
gobierna la lejanía.
De fondo la tristeza
del ave que no canta.
A gotas se desangra
un cielo gris de otoño.

---

[41] *Milvago chimango.* Ave rapaz que se distribuye desde Atacama a
Chiloé.

IN THE SHADOWS

An old and lame tiuque[42]
perches on my window.
It watches me slyly
presiding over the distance.
At heart the sadness
of the bird with no song.
A grey autumn sky
bleeds drop by drop.

---

[42] *Milvago chimango.* A bird of prey (resembling both the eagle and
the vulture) found between Atacama and Chiloé.

CHEMKÜN MAPU

Kaké narantü
Ka feychi anümka ka müten
Üngümniefí rüpü mew
Ka feychi wilu kürew ka müten.

PAISAJE

Cada tarde
El mismo árbol
Espera en el camino
La misma bandada de tordos.

LANDSCAPE

Every evening
The same tree
Waits in the path
Of the same flock of thrushes.

PERIMONTUN

Ñochíngechi pütókofin weñang
Mapu mew,
Ñámtükufin tañi kozáy may kallfü wenu mew
Ñi pelün kay mollfüñkünüwtuy.
Tañi züngún ellkáw ellkáwngelu pu kachu
Ñámkonpuy pu wayway püle ka pu waw püle lle nga.
Üyéchi küyen püchü malén ngelu nga iñche chalíkefuel
Tráfwünpafi chi pewman züngu
Wüñonaymekelu chemnomew.
Ñawe anay
Pienéw
Ngüfün ñi choyün
Impólmalayaymew tami foro epewün rayen.
Koñilerpuáy tami pu pewma.
Yükakifilngé chi pu ngüneltun rakíantü
Tami konünpaye la tuwün nielay,
Mawün engün choyütripaymí
Fey küme pewmalén
Tami trekán pelóntunerpuafí pun
Fey mi pünón rüpüluwürputuáy.
Ñawe anay
Kufíñ wenu wirár ngüláymaymew mi ngé
Fey élkünufem-meyu nga waw mapu mew
Welu küme niekan mi pu pewma
Tami nganél püchü malén ngelu llemay nga eymi.

Llükakilngé
Llegüyey tami kuwü mew
Koñíyeay tüfa pu epéwün rayen.

PERRIMONTUN[43]

Bebí la angustia de la tierra
lentamente,
hundí mi savia en el azul
y mi impulso fue sangre.
Mi voz oculta entre malezas
se perdió entre laderas y valles.
La luna que de niña saludaba
vino a besar anhelos
que se deshacían en la nada.
Hija mía
– me dijo –
no brotes de crepúsculos
cubrirán tus huesos las flores del alba.
Parirán tus sueños.
No temas a las horas marcadas
tu signo no es de muertos,
brotaste con las lluvias
anhelante
tu paso alumbrará la noche
y tu huella será el camino.
Hija mía
el grito de la aurora abrió tus ojos
y te abandoné en el valle,
pero guardo los sueños
que de niña sembraste.

No temas
ya brotan de tus manos
parirán ahora las flores del alba.

---

[43] Concepto que hace alusión a visiones y experiencias sobrenaturales
que le ocurren a la persona que debe iniciarse como *machi* (chamán
mapuche).

PERRIMONTUN[44]

I drank the anguish of the Earth
slowly,
I immersed my essence in the blue
and my impulse was blood.
My voice hidden in the weeds
lost in the foothills and valleys.
The moon I greeted as a child
rose to kiss desires
dissolving into nothingness.
Daughter
– it said –
do not come out at dusk
dawn flowers will cover your bones.
Dreams will give birth.
Do not fear the marked hours
your sign is not of the dead
you flowered with the rains
yearning
your steps will light the night,
your path will be the way.
Daughter mine
the cry of dawn opened your eyes
and I abandoned you in the valley,
but I keep the dreams
you sowed as a child.

Do not fear
they blossom from your hands
now the dawn flowers will give birth.

---

[44] A concept alluding to the visions and supernatural experiences of a
person initiated as a *machi* (Mapuche shaman).

LEMAWÜN

I.

Kurü mawünmekey nga fey wall mapu kay kiñe fütra
lewfületuy. Küyen ta ellkawmekeyiñmew fey ta pu laku
kuyfike züngu ta nentumekeyngün. Iñi norume pekan
epuzuamwümelay ñi pu nemül, tüfanurume femlayiñ,
ngoyünengewetulu Aguila pülom mew, alümapunefiel
üyechi pülpültuwe rüpü ta illkulen ka itro lladkülen
ngülalu deyiñentu mapu mew tüyechi epu peñiwen
Ignacio engü Belarmino Chiway. Tüyechi rüpü
ñangümfilu ñi pu peñi em fey Margarita kay matumatu
tranakünulu. Fachantü mawüni üyechi antü reke, itro
zumiñmaymapayiñmew taiñ pu nge.

II.

Kimwelan may iñche
Pinüfpüran ayongü rüpü püle.
Wüle wüñoan
– pin –
Fey patrüüan weke ül
Wümerkünuwün konümpayafiel.
Tüyemu may antü elkünuyefi
Tichi yapüz,
Tichi pu trafwün,
Ka chi petu arelechi pu koñiye
Ta we püñeñümum,
Tichi pu llellipun entulu ta iñche
Ka eypinolu ta iñche,
Tüyüw mawüzantü mew,
Tichi kürüf engü filu

Ñi püchürume wifkeñ,
Üyechi wengan rüpü pu triran wingkul mew.

Pun may ta
Kiñe fütra kura reke feley
Kallfüli we küyen
Ñi weñangkün reke.

HUIDA

I.

Llovía oscuro y el mundo era un inmenso lago. La
luna se ocultaba a nuestros ojos y los abuelos hablaban
de antiguos designios. Nadie dudaba entonces de sus
palabras, ni lo hacemos ahora, olvidados en el Valle
del Águila[45], alejados de la huella que con furia y saña
abrieron en la cordillera Ignacio y Belarmino Chiguay[46].
La misma ruta que perdió a sus hermanos y que
Margarita abandonó con premura. Llueve hoy como
entonces, oscuro ante nuestros ojos.

II.

Ajena yo
remonté por el camino claro.
Mañana volveré
– me dije –
y sembraré nuevos cantos.
Cerré los ojos para recordarlo.

Allí dejaba el sol,
la nieve,
los besos,
y las placentas aún calientes
de los últimos partos,

---

[45] La zona de Freire en la novena de región de Chile era nombrada
por los mapuches como Rukañanco o Casa del Aguila, un valle que
ahora es un territorio agrícola y ganadero ocupado por descendientes
de colonos y latifundistas.
[46] Nombres propios. Chiguay es un apellido mapuche que significa
"niebla o neblina".

las oraciones que dije
y las que no dije,
en la montaña,
el silbido agudo
del viento
y las culebras,
la ruta abierta en las quebradas.

La noche no es más
que una inmensa roca
azul como la melancolía
de la luna nueva.

FLIGHT

I.

It rained darkly and the world was an immense lake. The
moon hid from our eyes and our grandparents spoke of
ancient destinies. No one doubted their words, nor do
we now, forgotten here in Eagle Valley[47], far from the
track Ignacio and Belarmino Chiguay[48] opened viciously
and furiously in the Andes. The same route where
Margarita lost her brothers and which she abandoned
in haste. It rains now as it did then, darkly before our
eyes.

II.

Unaware
I went by the open trail.
Tomorrow I will return
– I told myself –
I will sow new songs.
I closed my eyes to remember.

There I left the sun,
snow,
kisses
and the still warm placentas
of recent births,
the prayers I said

---

[47] The Freire zone in the ninth region of Chile was named Rukañanco
or Casa del Aguila (House of the Eagle) by the Mapuches, a
valley that is now agricultural and cattle country occupied by the
descendants of colonists and latifundistas (owners of large estates).
[48] Chiguay is a Mapuche name that means "mist or fog".

and those I did not say,
in the mountain
the shrill whistle
of the wind
the snakes,
the open routes of ravines.

Night is nothing more
than an immense rock
blue as the melancholy
of the new moon.

TUWIN MALEN

Kurü wün mew lle tripalu ta iñche
Punwi ngünen ngen ka kolüwma ngen,
Pu pewma ñi pelün ngen
Ñamkülelu rüngefane mew,
Wümawkülechi ñüküf
Llitumum mongen ñi lafken mew,
Iñche may ta pun alof
Mangiñnelu tami mollfüñ

Küpange, rupafe fachi
Pelong ñi ngül antü
Fey fülümelen tami kewün ñi kochü poyen,
Trein tapül rayen fütrake kewlun engün,
Üyechi pu llampüdkeñ lewmawnefilu
Trokür engü kengzülla,
Pu tronge mawüzantü zumiñ
Lliwantunefilu chi perimol wangkülen.

Fülkonpange,
Welu atalükilnge
Kiñe püchü troy kafkünnurume
Amul-layaymi tañi zumiñ welling mew,
Üyüw itro punwikon ellkapuan ñi pu llükan.
Kake tramültramül llüpantükuniey kiñe lingafnag.
Kake llum züngu llitumongen ñi pu pilko

Kürüfngelu kay iñche ka lilngelu kay
Ka femngechi lig atrer rew üngalünelu rüf mupin
Ka müshke engü manshana ñi küme nümün ngen,
Achefkülen ka yallelün küyen wenu

Ka püzüm wangkülen
Pu pewma ñi mapu mew

Küpange, azkintupafe zumiñ tañi nge mew
Fey ñochingechi pütokofe
Kimfalnuchi züngu tañi kal longko mew
Tritrangkünun tañi pu mellfü ñi kimün
Adkintuyman tañi kalül ñi chülkü
Welu nülpüramüymakeli tañi
Ngeno konümpa üwe ñi impolwe.

TUWIN MALEN[49]

Porque yo desciendo del alba
instinto soy y delirio,
impulso de sueños
perdidos en la materia,
silencio dormido
en el mar del inicio,
yo la luz de la noche
que inunda tu sangre.

Ven, atraviesa
los siglos de la luz
y acércame la dulzura de tu lengua,
estallido de pétalos y llamaradas
mariposas huyendo de la niebla
y el eco,
oscuridad de selvas
aguardando la estrella del presagio.

Acércate,
pero no profanes
ni una nota de susurro
en mis abismos has de tocar,
allá en el fondo ocultaré mis temores.
Cada horizonte guarda una alborada.
Cada enigma las venas del origen.

Porque viento soy y peñasco
y ola blanca y fría que roe las certezas

---

[49] Espíritu mítico femenino mapuche. Habita en las lagunas. Allí enamora a los hombres desprevenidos y se los lleva a vivir a sus dominios.

y perfume de miel y manzano soy,
florido y fecundo cielo de luna
y estrellas desperdigadas
en la tierra de los sueños.

Ven, mira la oscuridad
en mis ojos
y bebe con lentitud
el misterio en mis cabellos
desnudo el saber de mis labios
mira el sello de mi cuerpo
pero no levantes el velo
de mi soledad sin memoria.

TUWIN MALEN[50]

I descend from the dawn,
I am instinct and delirium,
impulse of dreams
lost in matter,
silence asleep
in the sea of the beginning
the light of the night
inundating your blood.

Come, cross over
centuries of light
and draw nearer the sweetness of your tongue,
explosion of petals and flames
butterflies escaping the mist
and the echo,
darkness of forests
awaiting the heralding star.

Come closer
but do not defile
do not even murmur
you will touch the abyss within me,
and there in the depths I will hide my fears.
Every horizon contains a dawn.
Every enigma the veins of the origin.

I am wind and rock
and a cold, white wave that eats away certainties,
perfume of honey and apple,

[50] A Mapuche feminine mythological spirit that inhabits lagoons where
it seduces men, taking them by surprise to live in their domains.

flowering and fertile sky of moon
and scattered stars
in the land of dreams.

Come, watch the darkness
in my eyes
and drink slowly
the mystery in my hair,
the naked knowledge of my lips,
watch the form of my body
but do not lift the veil
of my solitude without memory.

WEZAKE PEWMA

I.

Pu illamkaye ñi chülkü engü kam pu llaypin,
fey fachi züngu mew pifal-lay, tremün rangiñkonkülen
tañi mollfüñ ñi üwümün züngu mew.

Ñi cheche, Manuel Curriao, llowenew tañi
ruka mew fey witruntükuy tañi püllü mew pu mongelyen
ñi kutrangkawün nowüngechi weychalelu engün
ñamnarwümenual.

Kizu ñi ñuke Margarita em püchü zomongelu
tripay üyechi pewen mapu mew. Witratunen tañi pu
mongen püñeñ ka ñizolnetew kiñe mülen che, tripay may
trawümen mapu püle.

"Wümawtukeyiñ may wente wükaf mamüll
mew, kiñe chellkom mew, kiñeke alluka traymanarümnel
müten..." eypiki ñi cheche fey shekütripayekey ñi pu
konümpa. Iñche ñochingechi püramtuken üyechi pu
epew kizu ta ngütramkalkefetew püchükechengelu nga
iñche ka ñi pu llamngen, petu ñi ngüñkün ka ñi katrün
fichi trülke nga witrantükuwe mawellal zewmafalngekelu
kake mapu püle.

Kizu ñi pewenche konümpa mangiñelfi ñi
püchüche mongen. Iñche tañi nge püle wiyuzyekey kizu
ñi pu epew ñi fentrenke cheyel: wefyeki filu, ngürü,
pangi, man püle wele püle mapunchezüngun ñi nemül,
kidu ñi kewün lle, kutranyefal kimeletew ta iñchiñ.

Kizu ñi pu pewma mu wallrupayekey
kom ñi pu mongeyel ka ñi pu wenüy -mongeleyelu
ka laleyelu- rakitulelatew ñi pu mongen engün: ñi pu
llüka, ñi pu weza antü ka ñi kizu kamapungetual, rumel

alümapulekefulu em. Margarita, mülekefulu müten
feychi wall mew, ngütramyekefi pu malle, pu laku, tañi
chaw. Rantuyekey ñi pu püñeñ. Kiñeke mew füken
mongewekey, kiñeke mew ngümakey… well züngukelay.
Alütripakey, ñüküfngechi yenetuel ñi illun wülzüngu.
Fentren mongen rupawüyey ñi pu kuwü
püle, welu pu mawüzantü ñi üwe mongen küpa el-layew.
Yapüz engü kütral may nga tañi pu trekan-
ngerputuy fachi pu alümapu waw püle.

II.

Achefün küla reke
Kam pun tatarün
Rupamekeyngün pu pewma
Azkünulu ñi kazi
Fachi füreke wiñalzüngu lle nga
Pun ñi upe mew.

Weñangkülüwngefuy tañi laku ñi pewma em
Yapüz üwe
Triran mawüza mew ka pu foro mew.

Weñangülüwngey tañi ñuke ñi pewma
Trümiñ kono müpafmüpafngelu
Trafyenefiel kürüf.

Welu zoy weñangülüwngey
Tañi pu püñeñ ñi pewma
Iñche tañi pu püñeñ ñi pu yall
Ngengenuchi mapu mew.

Wüle trongüpatuay mapu
Fütrake kuyfi filu em
Treng treng, kay kay

Fey nawnaway wenu
Taiñ wente longko mew ngati.
Femle nga
Pewün intas müleay
Fey may we küyen
Weke pewma mülegay
Fentrenke llampüzkeñ tramültramül püle.

Tüfa petu chemnorumengelayiñ
Ichu nurume
Dios taiñ ngollünetew
Ñi nge mew lle may nga.

MALOS SUEÑOS

I.

Con la marca de los despreciados o los
elegidos, que para el caso da igual, crecí bajo el designio
de mi sangre.

Mi abuelo, Manuel Curriao, me acogió en su
casa y vertió en mi espíritu el tormento de las estirpes
que luchan ferozmente por no extinguirse.

Su madre Margarita se vio alejada
tempranamente de las tierras del Pehuén. Con los
hijos vivos a cuestas y a cargo de un patrón de fundo,
emprendió el éxodo hacia la Frontera.

"Dormíamos sobre la viruta de la madera,
en una bodega, cubiertos con unos sacos..." dice mi
abuelo y se le llenan los ojos de recuerdos. Yo evoco con
ternura los relatos que de niños nos prodigaba a mí y
a mis hermanos, mientras curtía y cortaba cuero para
la confección de riendas que le encargaban de fundos
vecinos.

Su recuerdo pehuenche inundó mi infancia.
Desfilaban ante mis ojos los personajes de sus cuentos:
vilu, ñirre, pangui, a diestra y siniestra vocablos del
mapudungun, su lengua, que precariamente nos
entregaba.

En sus sueños circulaban todos los parientes y
los amigos – vivos y difuntos – para contarle de sus vidas:
sus temores, sus carencias y de su propia partida, siempre
lejana. Margarita, omnipresente en ese mundo, le habla
de los tíos, los abuelos, el padre. Pregunta por sus hijos. A
veces pide alimentos, a veces llora... a veces no habla. Se
aleja, llevándose en silencio los ansiados presagios.

Mucha vida ha pasado ya por sus manos,
pero la soledad de las montañas se ha negado a
abandonarlo.
Nieve y fuego han sido sus pasos por estos
alejados valles.

II.

Como quilas florecidas
o graznidos nocturnos
pasan los sueños
que formaron mi costado
amargos vaticinios
en la memoria de la noche.

Triste fue el sueño de mi abuelo
soledad de nieve
en las quebradas y en los huesos.

Triste el sueño de mi madre
oscura torcaza aleteando
contra el viento.

Pero más triste aún
el sueño de mis hijos
de los hijos de mis hijos
en territorio de nadie.

Mañana poblarán la tierra
las grandes sierpes de antaño
Treng Treng, Kai Kai[51]
y rugirá el cielo
sobre nuestras cabezas.

---

[51] Las serpientes de la tierra y del agua, respectivamente. Seres
míticos que libraron una feroz batalla en tiempos muy antiguos. Kai
Kai hizo crecer las aguas y Treng Treng aumentó la altura de los cerros
para que en ellos los mapuches se refugiaran y salvaran del diluvio.
En cada comunidad mapuche hay un cerro llamado Treng Treng, que
rememora a este ser mitológico.

Y luego
habrá brotes de cerezo
entonces luna nueva
nuevos sueños habrá
mariposas en el horizonte.

Por ahora nada somos
ni siquiera paja
en el ojo de Dios
que nos olvida.

BAD DREAMS

I.

With the mark of the scorned or the chosen ones, which in either case makes no difference, I grew up under the destiny of my blood.

My grandfather, Manuel Curriao, took me into his home and filled my spirit with the torment of lineages that fight ferociously against extinction.
His mother, Margarita, found herself removed early on from the lands of Pehuén. With her children on her shoulders and in charge of a landowner, she began her journey of exile towards La Frontera[52].

"We slept on wood shavings in a storeroom, covered with some sacks…" my grandfather tells us, and his eyes fill with memories. I recall with fondness the stories that he lavished on my siblings and me as children, while he tanned and cut the leather for the reins he made for neighbouring estates.

My childhood was flooded with his Pehuenche memories. Characters from his stories paraded before my eyes: vilu, ñirre, panqui, from left to right, Mapudungun words, his language, which he passed on to us precariously.

Relatives and friends, dead and alive, wandered through his dreams to tell him about their lives: their fears, their needs and of their own, always distant departures. Margarita, omnipresent in that world, tells him about aunts and uncles, grandparents,

[52] La Frontera is in the 9th region in Chile where the city of Temuco is located. It refers to the frontier which the Spaniards could not cross into Mapuche territory.

father. She asks after her children. Sometimes she asks for food, sometimes she cries... sometimes she remains silent. She leaves, taking with her in silence the longed-for premonitions.

Much life has passed through his hands, but the solitude of the mountains has not abandoned him.

Snow and fire have been his steps through these distant valleys.

II.

Like flowering quilas[53]
or nocturnal cawing
the dreams pass
that shaped my family
bitter prophecies
in the memory of night.

My grandfather's dream was sad,
solitude of snow
in the ravines and bones.

My mother's dream is sad,
dark dove flying
against the wind.

But even sadder
the dream of my children
of my children's children
in no-man's land.

Tomorrow they will populate the earth,
great serpents of long ago

---

[53] *Chusquea Quila*, a perennial bamboo that grows in the humid temperate forests of Chile and Argentina.

Treng Treng, Kai Kai[54]
and the sky will roar
above our heads.

And then
cherries will blossom
then a new moon
new dreams
and butterflies on the horizon.

For now we are nothing
not even straw
in the eye of God
who forgets us.

---

[54] Serpents of the land and water, respectively. Mythological beings
that waged a ferocious battle in ancient times. Kai Kai caused floods
and Treng Treng raised the height of the mountains so that the
Mapuches could find refuge and save themselves from the deluge.
In every Mapuche community there is a mountain called Treng Treng
that commemorates this mythological being.

PAULO HUIRIMILLA

WEYCHAFE ÜL

Iñche wariache nüfafe ñimitufe trülke tukun
Küllma longko lle may tripalu ta Pedro Eriazo
Ñi ataluwün mongen mew
Pu foro amulnefiel chi kiñe ellalkan ül
Ketro ketro züngun tañi pu laku em ñi pu la ñi zuam mew
Wükanel ñi illkun az
Ella zünguyawlu ñamümün
Tañi ngüneltükun üy.
Leliwülfin chi pu wezayma kintuyawületew ta iñchiñ
    pewma mew
Katrüfielmew chi pu trayapü ñi kürüf
Ka üyümkütralün mew "mamita virgen" ñi pu küze mew
Tüfa may züngumeken wichürkülen tañi wün kürüf ñi zuam
Trüngkaykantuyawün aflüfle wüla nga pitrun
Ka witrulerpule müten nga ko.
Wünümekefin chi aliwen lewfü mew kiñe wükan likan mew
Wüñokilpe püllomeñ üyechi kara üñüm engü
Weleyawlu pun mew
-rumel kangelu wefki üyechi azentu ñi wetron aywiñ mew-
Castilla züngun kam ngulü züngun chemnorume pepi
    eypikelay
Üye may witrukonkülepuy fichi rüngan mew chew ta
trüntrünkümekepumum ñi üngol
Iñche ta kizu engü trürküleken tañi püchüche mongen
    mew müten
Tüyechi antü mu chumul kiñe pültrükantuwe
    ükaftükuymakefetew ñi kuwü
Traf kochü fün mew
Itro achefkülelu trükoftükunel ñi pu folil
Femngechi may ta mongen che ñi allfeññgerpuy

Püramtunelu az lafken nampülkan cheñünen ñi nge
Fün mew
Ka taiñ pu foro ñi ülkantun kamapukünuwün.

CANTO DE GUERRERO

Yo cazador recolector urbano de chaqueta e' cuero
Pintado a la gomina nacido de la chingada[55]
De Pedro Eriazo[56]
Con una armónica música entre los dientes
Hablo tartamudo por los muertos de mis antepasados
Con el ceño partido
Parco de palabras se me ha perdido
El carnet de identidad.
Miro a los gangsters que nos buscan en el sueño
Por cortar el gas de los eucaliptos[57]
Y encender fuego con las velas de "mamita virgen"[58]
Hablo ahora torcida mi boca por el aire
Dando vueltas hasta que se queme el humo
Y el agua siga cayendo.
Estiro en el río el árbol con un trozo de licán[59]
Que la muerte no vuelva con aquel pájaro de la ciudad
Que augura de noche
— Siempre es el otro en el reflejo trizado de una fotografía —
La palabra Castilla o chileno nada puede expresar
Se vacía en el pozo en que la mordedura me tirita
Sólo puedo ser con ella en la infancia

---

[55] Chingar – mexicanismo que alude a dañar, protestar o perjudicar.
[56] Nombre propio, personaje del poema.
[57] Cortar el gas de los eucaliptos es un verso que alude a detener la siembra de eucaliptos en la zona mapuche de Malleco, donde grandes empresas forestales nacionales y extranjeras han plantado cientos de hectáreas con este árbol, junto a especies de pinares. Estos árboles dañan gravemente el ecosistema mapuche, contaminando la tierra y el agua proveniente de napas subterráneas.
[58] Así llaman los Huilliches, Mapuches de la décima región de Chile, a la Virgen María.
[59] Piedra pulida preciosa, mágica.

En que un columpio podría apretar mis manos
Junto al ciruelo
Florecido con la raíz hacia dentro
Es entonces la realidad una cicatriz del hombre
Que recuerda los viajes hacia el mar con una venda
En la semilla
Y la música de nuestros huesos hacia la muerte.

WARRIOR SONG

I, urban hunter and collector with leather jacket
Hair greased back, born of la Chingada[60]
Of Pedro Eriazo[61]
A harmonica between my teeth,
I speak with a stutter for the deaths of my ancestors
And a furrowed brow.
A laconic man I have lost
My identity card.
I see the gangsters who look for us in dreams
For cutting the gas of the eucalypts[62]
And starting fires with the virgin mother's candles.
I now speak with a crooked mouth in the air
Turning until the smoke burns
And the water keeps falling.
I stretch the tree in the river with a piece of licán[63]
So that death does not return with the city bird
That augurs in the night
"It is always the other in the cracked reflection of a
Photograph"
The Castilian or Chilean word
Expresses nothing
It disappears into a well in which my bite shivers
I can only be with her in my infancy

[60] A Mexicanism that means to damage, protest or harm.

[61] Personal name of the character in the poem.

[62] The line alludes to the prevention of the sowing of eucalypt trees in the Mapuche zone of Malleco, where the large forest companies, both national and foreign, have planted hundreds of hectares of this tree, together with species of pine. These trees gravely damage the Mapuche ecosystem and contaminate the earth and the subterranean water tables.

[63] A precious, polished stone with magical properties.

In a swing I could clutch with my hands
By the plum tree
Blossoming with its inward root
Hence reality is a man's scar
Remembering the journeys to the sea with a bandage
On the child
And the music of our bones toward death.

WÜÑOY TRIPANTÜ

Tüfa ñi rukangekefuy mapu ñi wenu mapu
Püray may chi kawell rügle pürapürawe mew
Tüfamu ta müley kom pu ñizol wüño
Pu kona ka chi newen:
– Ralün, Machikura, Kallfükura, Chewkelikan –
Münche zümiñ mew tripayey pu tokikura
Fa may witrungko kaiñpülekünuwtulu
Trayengko püle, lafken püle ka amuko püle
– Pewütunegafimi foye may fochüm ka triwe llemay ina
  kütral
Tüfa ta ka kiñe wallpan antüngetuay –
Llowken pu kapüra ñi piwke petu ñi lanon
Akuy ta Maywe püle tuwchi kiñe wewpife troyzüngupayal:
– Eypi – iñchiñ pu choyke kimtükufiyiñ malkokantun
Moymalltufiyiñ nga türompe engü wüño
Fichi kuram ñi ngeyku ta tremkülelu
Zoy nareltu ta tregül ñi müpüw mew
Welu fachantü fachi we tripan antü mew – eypi –
Rawillmangelayayiñ
Akuy nga püllü – eypi –
Pürugayiñ üyechi choyütripachi koñi reke
Fey püchay wüzatripalu ñi ñuke.

WIÑOI TRIPANTÜ[64]

Esta ha sido la casa del cielo de la tierra
El caballo sube hasta el séptimo peldaño
Aquí están todos los bastones de mando
Los mocetones y el poder:
– Ralün[65], Machikura[66], Kalfukura[67], Cheukelicán[68] –
Los toquicura[69] han salido debajo de lo oscuro
Es este el curso del agua que toma otro rumbo
Por vertientes, mares y esteros
– Debes cuidar hijo el canelo y laurel junto al fuego
Esta será otra vuelta de sol –
He recibido el corazón de los chivos antes de morir
Ha llegado un Wepife[70] de Maihue[71] a parlamentar:
– Dice – nosotros choique aprendimos el fútbol

---

[64] Nueva salida del sol. Año nuevo mapuche que se celebra en el momento del solsticio de invierno.

[65] Valle. Lugar cercano al seno del Reloncaví en la décima región de Chile. Existe allí una piedra sagrada para los mapuches de la zona.

[66] Piedra de la *machi* (chamán mapuche). Se trata de una piedra sagrada ubicada en el territorio de los pehuenches.

[67] Piedra Azul. Nombre de un famoso jefe militar mapuche de Argentina. Se da también este nombre a una gran piedra sagrada situada en un paso cordillerano que une Chile y Argentina en la zona sur.

[68] Piedra del *choike*. Roca sagrada ubicada en la comuna de San Juan de la Costa, Provincia de Osorno.

[69] Los *toquicura* eran insignias de poder y de mando de los *toquis*, jefes guerreros mapuches, hechas de piedra.

[70] Sabio mapuche, gran orador y conocedor de la historia de su pueblo, que él transmite a las nuevas generaciones.

[71] Localidad rural de la décima región de Chile, donde también hay un lago del mismo nombre.

Olvidado hemos el trompe[72] y el wiño[73]
El ritmo del huevo que crece más abajo
Que el vuelo del queltehue[74]
Pero hoy en esta nueva salida del sol – dice –
No seremos choroyes[75]
Ha llegado el espíritu – dice –
Danzaremos como la cría que nace y luego
Se desprende de su madre.

---

[72] Pequeño instrumento musical mapuche de metal, especie de diminuta arpa de boca. Posee una lengüeta que se hace vibrar con los dedos. La boca actúa como caja de resonancia.

[73] Palo curvo de madera dura que se utiliza en el antiguo deporte del *palín* o *chueca*, un juego que semeja al hockey sobre césped. Este juego aparece ya descrito por los primeros cronistas y conquistadores españoles.

[74] *Vanellus chilensis*. Ave conocida también con el nombre de treile o tregle. Se distribuye desde el valle de Copiapó hasta la isla de Chiloé. Los mapuches los consideran los guardianes de sus campos.

[75] *Enicognathus leptorhynchus*. Ave endémica de Chile semejante a un loro. Habita desde Aconcagua hasta Chiloé.

WIÑOI TRIPANTÜ[76]

This has been the house of the sky of the earth
The horse climbs up to the seventh step
All the batons of authority are here
The youth and the power
– Ralün[77], Machikura[78], Kalfukura[79], Cheukelicán[80] –
The toquicura[81] have come out from the darkness
This is the route of water that changes course
Through springs, oceans and brooks.
"You must care for the cinnamon tree and laurel, son,
Together with the fire
This will be another revolution of the sun"
I have received hearts of goats before death
A Wepife[82] from Maihue[83] has arrived to talk
He says us Choiques have learned football

---

[76] A new dawn. The Mapuche new year celebrated in the winter solstice.

[77] Valley. A place near the Reloncaví inlet in the tenth region of Chile, containing a rock that is sacred for the Mapuches of that area.

[78] Rock of the *machi* (Mapuche shaman). It refers to a sacred rock located in the territory of the Pehuenches.

[79] Blue Stone. Name of a famous Mapuche military chief from Argentina. This name is also shared by a giant sacred rock located in a mountain range pass that borders Chile and Argentina in the southern zone.

[80] Rock of the *choike*. A sacred rock located in the municipality of San Juan de la Costa, Osorno Province.

[81] The *toquicura* were insignia made of stone of the power and rank of the *toquis*, Mapuche war chiefs.

[82] A Mapuche wise man, great orator and scholar of the history of his people, which he passes down to future generations.

[83] A rural locality in the tenth region of Chile, where there is also a lake by the same name.

But have forgotten the trompe[84] and wiño[85]
The rhythm of the egg that grows below
The queltehue's[86] flight
But today in this new dawn – he tells us –
We will not be choroyes[87]
The spirit has arrived – he tells us –
We will dance like the newborn cub
That later parts from its mother.

---

[84] Small Mapuche musical instrument made of metal, a type of small mouth harp. It has a flexible tongue that is made to vibrate with the fingers. The mouth acts as a resonator.

[85] A curved pole made out of hard wood used in the ancient sport of *palín* or *chueca*, a game similar to hockey played on grass. This game is described by the first Spanish conquistadors and chroniclers.

[86] *Vanellus chilensis* (the Southern Lapwing, a large wader). A bird also known by the name *treile* or *tregle*. This bird is found from the Valley of Copiapó to the Island of Chiloé. The Mapuches consider this bird to be the guardian of their camps.

[87] Plural of *choroy* (*Enicognathus leptorhynchus*). Slender-billed Parakeet. A bird endemic in Chile similar to a parrot. It is found in the region from Aconcagua to Chiloé.

KOLLONG PÜRUN

Zewma petu tukuwüyen tañi kollong
Ka mallotukan ñi kalül tüyechi mallo kura mu ka trufken
   mu
Üytunefiel kallfü wenu ñi pu ñom
Püruyawün kiñe fütra püylawe ka ñi mamüll püchü
   kawell engü
Llafentuyawülfiel chi weküfü
Trayaytrayaytufin chi pu rüngi ta küme püllü inayatew
   ta iñchiñ
Yewün ñi küme felen müli tañi rakizuam mew
Yaom yaom yaom yaom
Yapuen yapuen yapuen yapuen
Arof engü konümpa, chemkün ñi pürun
Weychalerpun üyechi ñüküfnengechi züngu püle.

KOLLON PÜRRUN[88]

He comenzado a colocarme la máscara de kollón
y a pintarme el cuerpo nombrando los puntos del
    universo
con piedra mallo y ceniza.
Danzo con una espada y un caballito de madera
correteando al wekufü.[89]
Golpeo los coligües[90] para que el espíritu de la bonanza[91]
    nos siga.
El equilibrio de las cosas está presente en mi pensamiento
yaom yaom yaom yaom
yapuen yapuen yapuen yapuen[92]
sudor y memoria, la danza de los seres
la lucha desde lo silenciado.

---

[88] Literalmente significa "el baile del *kollón*". El *kollón* alude a una
máscara de madera que suele tener barba y bigotes. En el *nguillatún*,
ceremonial mapuche, el hombre que usa *kollón* resguarda el orden y
castiga a quienes no participan del ritual.
[89] Es un espíritu o fuerza del mal, que provoca desastres,
enfermedades y muerte.
[90] *Chusquea culeou*. Son gramíneas de tipo bambú, provistas de
cañas, a veces, de gran altura. Existe otra especie denominada
"quila" (*Chusquea quila, Chusquea cumingii*). Son especies frecuentes
y abundantes en los sotobosques y en los sitios afectados por la tala
de ecosistemas forestales. Los mapuches las utilizan para diversos
fines: cercas, muebles, construcción de casas, etc.
[91] Frase que hace referencia a un espíritu que trae todo lo bueno para
la vida mapuche.
[92] Gritos que se emiten para dar ánimo y energía vital y espiritual a
quienes bailan la danza del *choike*. También se profieren en ciertos
ceremoniales, como el *machitún* (ritual de sanación de un enfermo).

KOLLON PÜRRUN[93]

I've begun to put on the mask of kollón
and to paint my body naming the points of the universe
with white clay and ashes.
I dance with a sword and a wooden horse
in pursuit of wekufü.[94]
I hit the coligües[95] so that the spirit of bonanza[96] follows.
The balance of things is present in my thoughts
yaom yaom yaom yaom
yapuen yapuen yapuen yapuen[97]
sweat and memory, the dance of beings
the struggle of the silenced.

---

[93] Literally means the "dance of the kollón". The kollón refers to
a wooden mask that usually has a beard and moustache. In the
nguillatún, a Mapuche ceremony, the man that uses the kollón
maintains order and punishes those who do not participate in the
ritual.

[94] An evil spirit or force that brings disaster, sickness and death.

[95] Chusquea culeou (wild bamboo). A gramineous type of bamboo
that provides cane, sometimes of great height. There also exists
another kind called quila (Chusquea quila, Chusquea cumingii).
Chusquea species are prevalent and abundant in undergrowth and in
sites impacted on by the felling of forest ecosystems. The Mapuches
use them for a diverse range of ends: fencing, furniture, housing
construction etc.

[96] Refers to a spirit that brings all of the good things in Mapuche life.

[97] Cries emitted to encourage and give vital and spiritual energy to
those participating in the dance of the choike. They are also uttered
in ceremonies such as the machitún (a healing ritual for a sick person).

WENTEYAO ÑI PEÑI TAÑI ITRO LIG KAWELL

Pen kiñe kawell ta San Juan ñi eltun mew pi
Rüftu lig tüyechi wünman wunelfe reke
Tañi wente topel mew küpali
Santiago Wenteyao ñi peñi
Küpalneleyiñmew kiñe troy züngu
Ta wenu mapu püle tuwlu
Pefiel chumngechi ñi kachutukel külükintunetew ta iñchiñ
Kam chum ñi üngku witrapüraken fey
Ñi ngayngayüken kiñe tralkan reke
Tüfa tañi ellkawküleputun feychi malliñ mew
Kiñekemew ta pewfalüwkelu.

CABALLO BLANCO DEL HERMANO DE HUENTEYAO[98]

Dice ver un caballo en el cementerio de San Juan
blanco como un lucero que amanece.
Arriba de su lomo viene
el hermano de Santiago Huenteyao.
Una razón nos trae
desde la tierra de arriba.
Ver como pasta mirándonos de reojo
sin levantar cabeza
o bien pararse en sus dos pisaderas y
relinchar como un trueno
escondido ahora en la laguna
que a veces se nos aparece.

[98] Huenteyao es un espíritu benefactor de los mapuche-huilliches. La tradición indígena señala que habita un roquerío en el sector costero de Pucatrihue, provincia de Osorno. Ciertos relatos orales cuentan que Huenteyao adquirió la forma de un caballo blanco con alas y de este modo hizo frente a los conquistadores españoles.

BROTHER HUENTEYAO'S WHITE HORSE[99]

A horse is seen in the San Juan cemetery
white as a rising star.
Santiago Huenteyao's brother rides his back.
He brings a message
from the land of above.
See how he grazes watching us out of the corner of his eye
without lifting his head
or just stands on his two hind quarters and
neighs like thunder
hiding now in the lagoon
that is sometimes revealed to us.

---

[99] Huenteyao is the spiritual benefactor of the Mapuche-Huilliches. According to Indigenous tradition, he inhabits a rocky area in the coastal region of Pucatrihue, Osorno province. Oral histories tell that Huenteyao took the form of a white horse with wings to challenge the Spanish conquistadors.

AMUN TAÑI KUKU EM ÑI ELÜWÜN MEW

Pepun tañi fün ñi ange
Kimfalwenuchi metawe meñochallwalen
Kentraykülerputun ko mew
Petu ñi inafül antü püle rumenon
Katrünentunel kiñe kuwü lle may nga.

ASISTO AL ENTIERRO DE MI ABUELA PATERNA

Veo la cara de mi semilla
Cántaros cubiertos de peces
El viaje por el agua
Antes de pasar cerca del sol
Con una mano cortada.

I ATTEND THE BURIAL OF MY PATERNAL GRANDMOTHER

I see the face of my child
Water pitchers covered with fishes
The journey through water
Before passing near the sun
With a wounded hand.

ÜNGÜMKÜNEFUN ÑI AKUAEL KIÑE FÜTRA PÜLLÜ

Pewma püle narpatun.
Fachantü may trumiñ pun ngetuy fey ta pu anümka
makay trapekaw-wetulayngün
Kalmiñ mew tüngkülewepuy ko
Eymi kay kuyfi reke aychüfwelaymi anay, witranalwe.
Aywiñülüwmekefın tami kamapuyawün
Wünyelfe ñi llafinge mew.
Wüñopetupe pu lewfü
Kake lewfü ñi külleñü reke.

ESPERO LA LLEGADA DE UN GRAN ESPÍRITU

He bajado del sueño.
Hoy es noche de oscuridad y los árboles no se trenzan
las aguas se detienen en el musgo
y tú no brillas como antes, Witranalwe[100].
Reflejo tu ausencia en los párpados
del lucero.
Que los ríos vuelvan
como lágrimas de otros ríos.

---

[100] El Witranalwe según la tradición mapuche es el espíritu de un ser humano fallecido. Es un ser maléfico creado por un brujo mediante el manejo y control del "*alwe*" (alma de un difunto) y destinado a su servicio. También se denomina de este modo al *alwe* que regresa por propia iniciativa generalmente con propósitos maléficos.

I AWAIT THE ARRIVAL OF A GREAT SPIRIT

I have come down from my dream.
It is a dark night and the trees do not tangle their branches
the waters linger in the moss
and you do not shine as before, Witranalwe[101].
I reflect your absence in the eyelids
of the bright star.
May the rivers return
like tears of other rivers.

---

[101] According to Mapuche traditions, the *Witranalwe* is the spirit of someone who has passed away. It is an evil spirit created by a sorcerer via the domination and control of the *alwe* (soul of a dead person), destined to his service. This name is also given to the *alwe* that returns by its own initiative, usually with evil intentions.

PAYNE TRAYTRAYKO ÑI WÜYÜLCHE

Rumel müleki kizu tañi piwke mew
Tüye ta wünyelfe ñi pelotunielchi wüne nagchi mülfen.
Winüm wumekefi anümka ñi liken
Küyen ta zomo reke küpalkelu.
Kiñeke mew kimyekefi chi pu wapi chew ta pu challwa
Witrungko püle püypüytuwkünuwkelu engün
Llüfezkülen ñi pelong mew.
Pewmakefuy ñi kentrayküyawal
Kiñe payne traytrayko mew.
Ñüküfngechi
Tichi wüyülche witranagpuy kiñe arken tüngkentraywe
   mew
Chew ta pu kentraywe chapüz kuziforol ngemum
Ka chi kürüf kiñe kollongtulechi üñüm reke felemum.

EL NAVEGANTE DE LA CASCADA CELESTE

Siempre habita en su corazón
el primer rocío que el lucero alumbra.
Suele extender la plata del árbol
que la luna trae en forma de mujer.
Un día conoce islas en que peces
se orillan en esteros
por la luz de luminarias.
Ha soñado navegar
en una cascada celeste.
En silencio
el navegante atraca en un puerto seco
donde naves son de quillas planas
y el viento es como un pájaro con máscara.

NAVIGATOR OF THE CELESTIAL WATERFALL

The first dew lit by the morning star
always stays in his heart.
The silver of the tree extends
in the form of a woman brought by the moon.
One day he travels to islands where fish
edge the streams
in the luminescence of the lights.
He has dreamt of navigating
a celestial waterfall.
In silence
the navigator docks in a dry port
of flat-bottomed boats
and the wind is a masked bird.

ROXANA MIRANDA RUPAILAF

Akukayealu nga troy züngu
	Fey utrunentufin chi nüpüng tañi nge püle.
Tüfa ngeno neyen wirikameken
	Azkintunefiel
Chi pu waka rumenefilu chi kuykuy engün,
Chew ta allkeñngewenomum mamakün,
	Wirar may nga mületuy,
Tüyechi wayki ñi wirar üchafkonkülelu kazi mu ngati
Mollfüñ mu zichünefilu
Chi pu püllomeñ
Inayaetew engün ta iñche.

Wirikameken langümnewün ta iñche,
Pengelnefiel,
Ngüla allfeñmekel chew tañi pepi ngümayal
Fey trayaytükupuam fentrenke ruku mew.

Pütrün ngellipun may truürün mew.
Wirikameken lliwküzenmalen ñi pu nge.

Se cumple la profecía
                    y derramo la tinta por los ojos.
Escribo sin aliento
                    distrayéndome
en las vacas que atraviesan este puente,
en donde ya no se oyen mugidos,
                    sino gritos,
de una lanza clavada a la costilla
que señala con sangre
las muertes
que han de seguirme.

Escribo masacrándome,
mostrando,
abriendo llagas en que llorar
y golpear en tantos pechos.

Plegaria en los murmullos.
Escribo con velas en los ojos.

The prophecy is fulfilled
                and I pour ink from my eyes
I write without breath
                distracting myself
with the cows crossing this bridge,
where you no longer hear their bellows
                only the cries
of a spear stuck in the rib
that signals with blood
the deaths
to follow me.

Massacring myself, I write,
revealing,
opening wounds in which to cry
and to beat in so many chests.

Prayers among the murmurs.
I write with candles in my eyes.

MÜRWEN

Kiñe kawell wülli püle müpüwi rangiñ weychan mu.
Kiñe ngeno müpü kawell mañkaznelu kiñe tromü,
Ngütrümnenew tañi pu pewma ñi wüllngiñ mew
Chew ta kiñe awkangelu ta iñche zoy kolülu antü mew.
Ñomümfalnolu rakizuam reke,
Chingayün tañi puke amelzuam ta kachu nümün nielu
    engün.
Trepepüran.
Ütrünari may chi kawell wenu mapu püle
        Fey fükikünugenew.

PAREJA

Un caballo vuela al sur en medio de la guerra.
Un caballo sin alas montado en una nube,
me llama a la puerta de mis sueños
donde soy una potra más rubia que el sol.
Indomable como un pensamiento,
relincho mis ilusiones con olor a hierbas.
Despierto.
El caballo se cae del cielo
              y me deja preñada.

PARTNER

A horse flies south in the midst of battle.
A horse without wings mounted on a cloud,
calling me to the door of my dreams
where I am a filly blonder than the sun.
Indomitable as a thought
I whinny my illusions with an aroma of herbs.
I wake up.
The horse falls from the sky
                and leaves me pregnant.

IÑCHE YAFKAFE

Entuzünguan tañi weñeymafiel Cristo ñi piwke ñi am,
Tañi furi püle langümfiel kiñe rayen
Ka tralkatufiel chi piwkansu.
Entuzünguan
Tañi kom iyfiel chi müshki
Ka tañi külachi afkizuamkel
Üypürayüm chi küyen.
Koylatulelfiel ta ngeno werin
Ka tañi kupafüfiel tichi küme piwke.
Entuzünguan tañi illukefiel ñi pu trafche
Ka tañi niel wedake rakizuam
                    Kiñe santito engü.
Entuzünguan tañi wülüwün liken ñi zuam.
Ta iñche ngenon
Ka tañi rakizuam mu werikel
                    nemül ka kiñepülekünuwün mew.
Fey eypian tañi türpu katrüzuamnon.

YO PECADORA

Confieso que le he robado el alma al corazón de Cristo,
que maté una flor por la espalda
y le disparé a la cigüeña.
Confieso
que me comí todas las manzanas
y que suspiro tres veces
al encenderse la luna.
Que le mentí a la inocencia
y golpeé a la ternura.
Confieso que he deseado a mis prójimos
y que tengo pensamientos impuros
                           con un santito.
Confieso que me vendí por dinero.
Que no soy yo
y que he pecado de pensamiento
                      palabra y omisión.
Y confieso que no me arrepiento.

I, SINNER

I confess that I stole the soul of Christ's heart
that I killed a flower from the back
and shot the stork.
I confess
that I ate all the apples
and that I sigh three times
when the moon rises.
That I lied to innocence
and pounded tenderness.
I confess that I have desired my neighbours
and that I have impure thoughts
                    about a certain saint.
I confess that I sold myself for money.
That I am not me
and have sinned in thought
                    word and omission.
And I confess that I do not repent.

KARÜ

Llangkonagwümey nga pu tapül tañi kalül mew
Fey ta meñolingün katrüntuku ruka weñangkün mew.

Tritrangkülen,
Antü küpa kontupulanew tañi azkintutripawe püle.

Llikozkülen tañi pu foro mew lay chi kiñe üñüm.

Kürüf ta wenu ruka püle wülelküyawülenew puliwen mew.

Lukutulen, ngeno nemülkünuenew may chi mamülltufe.

VERDE

Las hojas se fueron cayendo de mi cuerpo
e inundaron la pieza de nostalgias.

Desnuda,
el sol no quiso entrar por mi ventana.

Acurrucado entre mis dientes murió un pájaro.

El viento me golpea contra el techo en las mañanas.

De rodillas, me deja el leñador sin las palabras.

GREEN

Leaves went falling from my body
and drowned the room in nostalgias.

Naked,
the sun chose not to come through my window.

Curled up between my teeth a bird died.

The wind beats me against the roof in the mornings.

Kneeling, the woodcutter leaves me without words.

PU LLAMPÜZKEÑ KAWELLUTUNEFINGÜN KIÑE PESHKIÑ...

Tichi pu llampüzkeñ kawellutunefingün kiñe peshkiñ
Münche fichi puke müpü mu tremyelu
Ko ñi ülkantun mew.

Tüyechi pu wümawmu takuwingün
Kürüf ta kiñe püylawe mu
Katrüyawül-lu küyen ñi inarüpü püle.
Tichi pu llampüzkeñ itro küme nümüneyngün ñi puke
    kürpu engün
Ta ellka trawülüwkeyüm mew antü engün llemay.

Kizu engün kushenagkeyngün azkintunefiel pu wangkülen
Nielu ta kiñe müñawpürache.

Pütokonefingün üyechi relmu katrürumefilu
Kiñe püchü kampu ñi furi petu ñi müpüwkülen.
Layüm chi pu llampüzkeñ
Llompüpuketuy tami am mew.

LAS MARIPOSAS CABALGAN UNA FLOR...

Las mariposas cabalgan una flor
bajo las alas que crecieron
de la canción del agua.

Se visten de los sueños
que el viento con cuchillo
anda cortando en las veredas de la luna.

Las mariposas llevan los senos perfumados
de los encuentros secretos con el sol.

Ellas envejecen mirando las estrellas
que posee un vagabundo.

Beben el arco-iris que cruzó
la espalda de un niño en pleno vuelo.
Las mariposas cuando mueren
emigran a tu alma.

BUTTERFLIES RIDE A FLOWER...

Butterflies ride a flower
under wings that grew
from the water's song.

They dress in dreams
the wind cuts with a knife
along the sidewalks of the moon.

The breasts of butterflies are perfumed
by their secret liaisons with the sun.

They age gazing at the stars
owned by a vagabond.

They drink the rainbow that crossed
the back of a child in full flight.
When butterflies die
they migrate to your soul.

ÜNGÜMNEFEL TAÑI AYÜN

Zewma iñangeküley tañi ayün,
Epu wüzan ka mari kechu püchü troy antü llemay.

Zünguafin tañi ngütrümtuwe mew.

Inanewüyen rüpü pi.

¿azkülepey may ñi ange?

¿ayüpeay may ñi we yiwüzrayeñ
nümün?

¡tüyüw ta küpali!

Tüyechi inangüman wechumün pewma ñi furi wüllngiñ
püle.
Ülkantulerpan, tañi kamapungetual.

ESPERANDO AL AMANTE

Se ha retrasado mi amante,
2 horas y 15 segundos.

Voy a hablarle al celular.

Dice que viene en camino.

        ¿Estará bien mi maquillaje?

        ¿Le gustará mi nueva fragancia
        de calas?

                ¡Allá viene!

Tras el umbral del último sueño cumplido.
Cantando, mi muerte.

WAITING FOR MY LOVER

My lover is late,
2 hours and 15 seconds

I call him on my mobile.

He says he's on his way.

> Will my make-up be OK?

> Will he like my new perfume of
> Arum Lilies?

> Here he comes!

Behind the threshold of the last fulfilled dream,
Singing, my death.

Ütrünaryüm ta che
Entutakuwki tati ka pewki ñi am engü,
Uwamngeki llamllamtripan zañe mu
Ka üyechi pu ngeno müpüw üñüm ñi wirar
Pewmanefilu ongto mongen engün punwikon püzo mew.

Kürüf züngun: merüf tükun.
Neyüntükunefiel kakelu ñi pitrun.

Ütrünarün nga che az lululwenu püle ngeno tichi
   pewmakefuel chi pewma,
Püchükeyma longkontükunefiel pelong.

Caer
es desvestirse y encontrarse con el alma,
sentir emigraciones del nido
y el grito de los pájaros sin vuelo
 que sueñan la eternidad en el fondo del ombligo.

 Diálogos de aire: boca nadas.
Respirando hacia dentro los humos de los otros.

Caer del infinito sin el sueño soñado,
con huellas de luz en la memoria.

To fall
is to undress and meet with your soul,
feel the migrations from the nest
and the cry of flightless birds
     dreaming eternity in the depths of the navel.

      Dialogues of air: puffs.
Breathing in the smoke of others.

Fall from infinity without the dreamt dream,
traces of light in memory.

JAIME LUIS HUENÚN VILLA

RAUQUEMO PIWKAN

Kintuyawülkeyiñ lawen lelfün püle
(ngüchayngüchay engü polew, üllfaw engü pilluñiweke).
Koñillküleki antü, trangliñnarki kachu.
Zumiñkülen narkonküleki Ragwe zew aychüfwenon pu
    challwa.

Allküyiñ ta mamakün pu waka ñamküyawlu rulu mew
Ka kiñe witrawe pañillwe ñi rünrünün amulelu
    Cancha Larga püle.
Puwiyiñ chi lewfü mu fey fükepuyiñ wüllfü;
Kiñe tangi ñüküfkülen wütupayiñmew.

Kafkü züngueyiñmew fey elueyiñmew ükon
Ka kiñeke alim kolka pülku yeafiüm chi wütre.
Matumatu weyülüyiñ trüküfnuam.
Trokür nga nürüfnefi chi püll lewfü.

Rangi rüme nga epu kochüko kalül,
Rüftu lig epu küyen reke pu ko pun mew,
Malangkünuyngü ñi epu wechoz ngüchayngüchay pel,
Türpu küzawtunon kiñepülekünuyemekefiel tichi pu
    litraf ka chi mangiñ ko.

Kake külentukünufingün kam namuntukünufingün chi
    üñüm
Fey tangi püle küpay ellkawkülerpan pu anümka mew.
Pu wentru may üyümingün ñi nüfawe küze
Fey allukatulen ütrüfnentufingün chi epeke la nüfa.

Ngollilen amutuyiñ, püllomeñ pichuñmanewel,
Ülkantunerpufiel kiñeke küfche ül ka willitulerpuel
   kürüf mew.
Rangiñ lelfün wümawnagiyiñ
Fey impolnangümeyiñmew trangliñ, kachu ka ünfi llemay.

CISNES DE RAUQUEMÓ

Buscábamos hierbas medicinales en la pampa
(limpiaplata[102] y poleo, hierbabuena y llantén[103]).
El sol era violeta, se escarchaban los pastos.
Bajaba el Rahue[104] oscuro ya sin lumbre de peces.

Oímos mugir vacas perdidas en la vega
y el ruido de un tractor camino a Cancha Larga.
Llegamos hasta el río y pedimos balseo;
un bote se acercó silencioso a nosotros.

Nos hablaron bajito y nos dieron garrotes
y unos tragos de pisco para aguantar el frío.
Nadamos muy ligero para no acalambrarnos.
La neblina cerraba la vista de la orilla.

En medio del junquillo dos cuerpos de agua dulce,
blancos como dos lunas en la noche del agua,
doblaron sus dos cuellos de limpia plata rotos,
esquivando sin fuerzas los golpes y el torrente.

Cada uno tomó un ave de la cola o las patas
y remontó hacia el bote oculto entre los árboles.
Los hombres encendieron sus linternas de caza
y arrojaron en sacos las presas malheridas.

---

[102] *Equisetum arvense*. Tipo de helecho con propiedades medicinales (diurético, cicatrizante y astringente dermatológico).

[103] *Plantago major L.* Planta que crece en forma de maleza y que tiene diversos usos medicinales (propiedades emolientes, hemostáticas, diuréticas, astringentes y desinfectantes).

[104] Río que atraviesa la ciudad de Osorno. La palabra Rahue significa "lugar de la greda", un tipo de arcilla que los mapuches utilizan para fabricar vasijas y otros utensilios.

Nos marchamos borrachos, emplumados de muerte,
cantando unas rancheras y orinando en el viento.
En mitad de la pampa nos quedamos dormidos
cubriéndonos de escarcha de hierba y maleficios.

RAUQUEMÓ SWANS

We searched for medicinal herbs in the pampas
(limpiaplata[105] and pennyroyal, mint and llantén[106]).
The sun was violet, the grass covered in frost.
Rahue[107] flowed dark without the light of fish.

We heard the bellows of cows lost in the market
and the noise of a tractor on the road to Cancha Larga.
We arrived at the river and called for a ferry,
a boat drew near in silence.

They spoke in hushed voices and gave us clubs
with sips of pisco for the cold.
We swam quickly to avoid cramp.
The mist enshrouded the bank.

Amid the rushes two bodies of sweet water
white like two moons in the night river
bending their two necks of broken silver
defenceless against the blows and the torrent.

Each of us took a bird by the tail or feet
and headed to the boat hidden in the trees.
Men lit their hunting lanterns
throwing the wounded prey into sacks.

---

[105] *Equisetum arvense.* (Scouring Rush). A type of fern with medicinal properties (diuretic, healing and dermatological astringent).

[106] *Plantago major L.* A plant that grows like a weed and has a range of medicinal uses (with emollient, haemostatic, diuretic, astringent and disinfectant properties).

[107] A river that crosses the city of Osorno. The word Rahue means "place of clay", a type of clay used by Mapuches to make earthenware vessels and other utensils.

We marched drunk, feathered in death
singing folk songs and pissing in the wind.
In the middle of the pampa we fell asleep
covered in grass, frost and curses.

ANAHÍ TA WERKÜLELNGEL ZÜNGU

Wünkülewüyerkey fey iñche
Turayen küyawül-leyu tañi pu püllü züngu chillka mew.
Wif mawünüy may wente mapu, tañi pewma mu kay
Ngülayey wüne kelüke choyün zengüll.
Mawüzantü püle müpüwingün pu wayraw
Fey tue - tue kay külachi zünguy
Re tañi keñanatew müten.
Wünmam wüla ngati: llampüzkeñngerki wenu,
Marangerki nga mapu inalefnefiel chi antü.
Püchüymamew pewümeyu nga pomomümeken inafül
    müshke llemay,
Rawmeken
Tami ñuke ñi lig impolkoñiwe mew.
Tichi püllomeñ ta
Ko ñi wirintükukel wente ko lle tati, eypiwün azkintunefiel
Feychi pu tapül ñi mülfen.
Ngüman, ngüman may
Re tañi fentre ayüfiel müten ñi neyüneal tami kürüf.

ENVÍO A ANAHÍ

Era madrugada y yo
cortaba flores para ti en mis libros de poesía.
Llovió largo sobre el mundo y en mi sueño
se abrieron los primeros rojos brotes de poroto.
Hacia el bosque volaron los güairaos[108]
y el tué-tué[109] cantó tres veces
sólo para confundirme.
Amanecí después: mariposa era el cielo,
liebre era la tierra corriendo tras el sol.
Te vi luego zumbando en las orillas de la miel,
haciendo olas en la blanca
placenta de tu madre.
La muerte es lo que escribe
el agua sobre el agua, me dije contemplando
el rocío de las hojas.
Lloré, entonces lloré,
sólo por el delirio de respirar tu aire.

---

[108] *Plural de güairao*, ave nocturna también conocida como *huairavo* (*Nycticorax nictycorax*). Posee un plumaje oscuro y un graznido ronco y atemorizador. Para los mapuches es un ave de mal agüero.

[109] Pájaro mítico mapuche, también llamado "*chon-chón*". El *tué-tué* es un pájaro nocturno que, según los mapuches, es un brujo que en las noches desprende la cabeza de su tronco para volar. Se trata, entonces, de una cabeza humana con alas, que en realidad son enormes orejas. Las creencias indígenas señalan que quien escucha el canto del tue-tué, inevitablemente sufrirá grandes desgracias.

LETTER FOR ANAHÍ

It was dawn
and I cut flowers for you in my books of poetry.
It rained long over the land and in my dream
the first red buds of beans opened.
The güairaos[110] flew toward the forest
and the tué-tué[111] sang three times
only to confuse me.
Later I awoke; the sky was a butterfly
and the earth a hare chasing the sun.
I saw you buzzing around the edges of the honey
making waves in your mother's
white placenta.
Death is what water writes
on water, I told myself, contemplating
the dew on the leaves.
I cried, then I cried,
only for the delirium to breathe your air.

---

[110] Plural of *güairao*. A nocturnal bird also known as *huairavo* (*Nycticorax nictycorax;* Black-Crowned Night Heron). It has a dark plumage and a harsh, frightening squawk. For the Mapuches this bird is a bad omen.

[111] Mythical Mapuche bird, also known as the *chón-chón*. The *tué-tué* is a nocturnal bird that, according to the Mapuches, is a sorcerer that during the night detaches its head from its body to fly. It consists of a human head with wings, that in reality are enormous ears. According to to Indigenous beliefs, whoever hears the song of the *tué-tué* will inevitably suffer great misfortune.

PÜRUN[112]

Inche ta leliwülnefin
Pürumeki
Rayün foye lleniey tañi pu kuwü mew
Pürumeki
Ñi püchüke namun itro peleymalen
Pürumeki
Ngülngu rayen ka müshke yeniey ñi longko mew
Pürumeki
Ayey ka püruy
Pütokonerpuy ñi muzay
Iñche ta leliwülnefin
Iñche ta püruwümelan
Fey tichi pürun ñi trufürpüramchi tafü
Penchuntukünuenew
Kizu ñi nge mew.

---

[112] Tüfa mew ta fentren che kiñentrür amulki ñi pürun
ngillatunmungepe kam kake mapuche trawün mew.

PURRÚN[113]

Yo la miro
danza
canelo florecido lleva en sus manos
danza
sus pequeños pies llenos de tierra
danza
flores del ulmo y miel en su cabello
danza
ríe y danza
bebe su muday[114]
yo la miro
yo no danzo
y el polvo que levanta el baile
me oculta
ante sus ojos.

---

[113] Baile colectivo usado en el "*nguillatún*" y otros ceremoniales.
[114] Bebida mapuche fabricada en base a trigo o maíz y miel. Se puede tomar como refresco o como bebida alcohólica una vez fermentada.

PURRÚN[115]

I watch her
she dances
with cinnamon flowers in her hands
she dances
her small feet covered in dust
she dances
with honey flowers in her hair
she dances
she laughs and dances
she drinks her muday[116]
I watch her
I do not dance
and the dust rising from the dance
hides me
before her eyes.

---

[115] A collective dance used in the "nguillatún" and other ceremonies.
[116] A Mapuche drink made from a base of wheat or honey and maize.
It can be drunk as a soft drink or, once fermented, an alcoholic drink.

VÍCTOR LLANQUILEF NGOLLILEN RÜLTRENEFI CHI TANGI PU WAMPU LEWFÜ PÜLE

Kiñe koypu weyülküyawi antü mew
Eymi kay ngilakonimi ko mew, ñochingechi.
Tami inapülengerputuy tichi troypoko rüme engü
Ka chi pu sauce ñi alürupa llawfeñ
Femngechi feletual tami llawfeñ münche ko.
Kiñe challwa witrampüramüy pelong wente yufü mew.
Tüyechi ülef tami püllürke ngati
Ka wüño ñamkonkületulu itro punwikon mew.

153

VÍCTOR LLANQUILEF EMPUJA EL BOTE EBRIO AL RÍO DE LAS CANOAS

Un coipo[117] nada en el sol
y tú te recoges en el agua, silencioso.
Son tus orillas el berro y el junco
y la ancha sombra de los sauces
el destino de tu sombra bajo el agua.
Un pez alza la luz sobre el remanso.
El destello es tu espíritu
que se hunde en lo profundo

                              nuevamente.

---

[117] *Myocastor coypus*. Es el roedor más grande de la fauna chilena.
Habita ríos, lagos y lagunas de la zona central y sur del país.

VÍCTOR LLANQUILEF LAUNCHES THE DRUNKEN BOAT INTO THE RIVER OF CANOES

A coypu[118] swims in the sun
and you withdraw into yourself in the water, silent.
Your banks are watercress and reeds
and the wide shadow of the weeping willow,
the destiny of your shadow under the water.
A fish lifts light to the pool's surface
the flash is your spirit
that disappears into the depths

                                                    again.

---

[118] *Myocastor coypus.* The largest rodent of Chilean fauna. It inhabits rivers, lakes and lagoons in the central and southern region of the country.

JOSÉ MARÍA HUAIQUIPÁN AWÜYAWI ÜYÜW WENU LEWFÜ PÜLE

Ngümayerkenew ñi pu zomo ka ñi pu trem
Üyechi püramuwün küyen mew.
Lay pirkenew lelfün püle wirarkülen engün
Petu ñi katrüel mapu kachilla engün
Iñche tañi kuwü nganlu lle nga.
Pen tañi mongen tralka mu pawküneymangel
Ka traymanagümneymangel üyechi walüng pu rayen mew.
Pen tañi mollfüñ kimngewetunon
Tachi kawell ñi mollfüñ mew tüfa ta wente ko
mañkazküyawültulu ta iñche.
Mollfüwelan fey zoy weche wentruletun fachi kürüf mew
Wente lewfü ta witrampüramkünelu tañi kawell.
Kimwetulan tañi ruka tichi pu mawüzantü norume
Pun lle nga ngollilen katrürupafilu iñche.
Pu anümka ñi ülkantun müten allkütunen
Chew ta wümawkülemum antü ñi puke üñüm.
Ka pu wentru ñi züngun üyechi pu tangi mew
Meñolelu waka mew ka püchüke wüfiza mew.
Kizu engün ta azkintuymanew ñi ayong ange
Chew aychüfkülemum pu narantü wangkülen.
Kizu engün ta azkintuymanew ñi llawfeñ
Üyechi püz puke ko mew narkülelu lafken püle.

JOSÉ MARÍA HUAIQUIPÁN[119] CABALGA EN CÍRCULOS SOBRE EL RÍO DE LOS CIELOS

Me han llorado mis mujeres y mis padres
en el mes de las cosechas.
Que me he muerto gritan ellos en las lomas
mientras cortan los trigales
sembrados por mi mano.
Vi mi vida reventada por las balas
y cubierta por las flores de febrero.
Vi mi sangre confundirse con la sangre
del caballo que ahora monto sobre el agua.
Ya no sangro y soy más joven en el viento
que levanta mi caballo sobre el río.
No recuerdo ya mi casa ni los bosques
que de noche atravesé borracho.
Sólo escucho el canto de los árboles
donde duermen los pájaros del sol.
Y las voces de los hombres en las lanchas
atestadas de vacunos y corderos.
Miran ellos mi cara transparente
donde brillan las estrellas de la tarde.
Miran ellos mi sombra en la espesura
de las aguas que bajan hacia el mar.

---

[119] Nombre propio. Huaiquipán es nombre mapuche que significa
"lanza del puma".

JOSÉ MARÍA HUAIQUIPÁN[120] RIDES IN CIRCLES OVER THE RIVER OF THE SKIES

My women and parents have mourned me
in the month of the harvest.
They cry my death in the hills
as they cut the wheat
sown by my hand.
I saw my life riddled with bullets
and covered in the flowers of February.
I saw my blood mix with the blood of the horse
that I now ride over the water.
I no longer bleed and I am younger in the wind
that lifts my horse over the river.
I no longer know my house nor the woods
I crossed on drunken nights.
I only hear the songs of trees
where the birds of the sun sleep.
And the voices of men in their boats
crowded with lambs and cattle.
They look at my transparent face
where the evening stars shine.
They look at my shadow in the thickened waters
flowing down to the sea.

---

[120] Mapuche personal name. Huaiquipán is the Mapuche name for
"leap of the puma".

ELUWÜN

Fachi pu ko tañi allush kürüf, Elías Huenún,
Ezequiel rüngalkülelu Osorno ñi llüngüz mapu püle.
Kom tañi pu kuñülyen küme nüwküleyngün lewlew mew,
Luyüfküleyelu engün tichi pu üñfitun ñi milla mew.
Eypiayu may, fochüm, tañi pewmael Herminda engü.
Küparki nga yepayatew kureyeagelchi domo reke
   tukuwtulen.
Amuyu, pienew, üyüw iñche tañi mülemum,
Itro fill wüme kümelkali fey chemnorume afmakelan.
Femlu fey fülmapaenew mufü zumiñ püchükeche,
Tofkütuymanew ñi ange engün petu ñi añütumeken.
Kiñe triwkü chi lawal wente ruka mew zewmapay ñi zañe,
Tañi laku llafentufi ko mew ka lliwüm chazi mew.
Fachi pu ko tañi allush kürüf, Elías Huenún,
Fülkonpamün tachi mapu püle kümkümpürakelu pun mew,
Fachi rünganko püle, ruka achawall püle, tachi ligke
   manzano püle,
Tachi pu keltawma ñi yawaw kultraftunefilu mutrung
   mapu püle.
Tañi ruka renulelu wente millawmaye liken,
Tañi ruka witrampüramkülelu wente kütral engü filla,
Tañi ruka pelotunetew züchüke kawell,
Tañi ruka ngülakünulelfi wüllngïñ tüyechi püllomeñ ka
   chi kurüwün.
Tüfa may Francisca Huenún ngetuy ta rüngalkonkületulu
Leliwülnetew ta iñche rangiñ rayen ka üykülechi küze püle.
Wekun ta trekayawingün pu kuñülyen fey
Nüfülneluwingün pülku, ti ilo, chi pu nemül.
Ñi tükukan tañi ñuke puliwen engü amutuy.
Inageyew pu intas, pu sauce, pu tralemküwe.

Tañi pu wümaw ñi ñüke, püchütrem fey rüngalkonkületulu,
Yomelelürpuenew tañi ürkükawün llawfeñ.
Eypiayu may, fochüm anay, ñefñef tañi pekeel
Narkületun tañi ngütantu püle we pürapachi antü mew.
Feymu lle welu wirikawkakünuwken kütral mu ka
    trufken mu
Ka ngillatuiñmakakünuken ñi tol ko mu ka ngellipuiñma
    chazi mu.
Fachi pu ko tañi allush kürüf, Elías Huenún,
Catalina, Zulema, Carlos, Margarita,
Kom tañi pu mollfüñ kake pun üytunefiel
Mapu mew ka ñamkületuchi pu mawüzantü ñi kengzülla
    mew.

ENTIERROS

Aura de las Aguas, Elías Huenún,
Ezequiel enterrado en los llanos de Osorno.
Todos mis parientes aferrados a las llamas,
bruñidos por el oro de las hechicerías[121].
Te diré , hijo mío, que soñé con Herminda.
Venía ella a buscarme vestida como novia.
Vamos, me decía, allá donde yo vivo,
todo es tan bonito y no me falta nada.
Después se me allegaron unos niños oscuros,
la cara me escupieron entre sueño y vigilia.
Un tiuque[122] hizo su nido en el techo de alerce,
mi nieta lo espantó con agua y sal batida.
Aura de las Aguas, Elías Huenún,
acérquense a la tierra que arde por las noches,
al pozo, al gallinero, a los blancos manzanos,
al ruido de cadenas chocando en los cimientos.
Mi casa levantada sobre el oro y la plata,
mi casa construída sobre fuego y miseria,
mi casa iluminada por caballos fantasmas,
mi casa abrió su puerta a la muerte y al alba.
Ahora es Francisca Huenún la que yace
mirándome entre flores y cirios encendidos.
Afuera los parientes caminan y se pasan
de mano en mano el vino, la carne, las palabras.
La madre de mi huerto se va con la mañana.
La siguen los cerezos, los sauces, las campanas.
La madre de mis sueños, pequeña y enterrada,

---

[121] Brujerías, encantamientos por medio de poderes oscuros.
[122] *Milvago chimango*. Ave rapaz que se distribuye desde Atacama a Chiloé.

me deja como herencia su sombra fatigada.
Te diré, hijo mío, que he visto sabandijas
bajando de mi cama apenas raya el día.
Por eso me hago cruces de fuego y de ceniza
y santiguo mi frente con agua y sal bendita.
Aura de las Aguas, Elías Huenún,
Catalina, Zulema, Carlos, Margarita,
todos mis hermanos nombrados noche a noche
en la tierra y el eco de montañas perdidas.

BURIALS

Aura of the Waters, Elías Huenún,
Ezekiel buried in the plains of Osorno.
All of my relatives sitting around the fire,
burnished in the gold of enchantments[123].
I will tell you, son, I dreamt of Herminda.
Dressed as a bride she came to find me.
Let's go, she said, over there where I live,
everything is so beautiful and I want for nothing.
Later some dark children gathered around me
and spat on my face between dream and wakefulness.
A tiuque[124] made its nest in the larch roof
my granddaughter scared it away with a mixture of salt
    and water.
Aura of the Waters, Elías Huenún,
come to the land that burns in the night,
to the well, the chook house, the white apple trees,
to the noise of chains crashing in the foundations.
My house built on gold and silver
my house built on fire and misery
my house lit by the phantom horses
my house opened its door to death and the dawn.
Now it's Francisca Huenún laid out there
watching me through flowers and candles.
Outside my relatives walk and pass
hand to hand the wine, meat and words.

---

[123] Sorcery and enchantments by means of dark forces.
[124] *Milvago chimango.* A bird of prey (resembling both the eagle and
the vulture) found between Atacama and Chiloé.

The mother of my garden, leaves with the morning.
Cherry trees, willows and bells follow her.
The mother of my dreams, small and buried,
leaves me the inheritance of her tired shadow.
I will tell you, son, that I have seen the vermin
crawling from my bed in the first light of dawn.
This is why I cross myself with fire and ash
and holy water and salt on my brow.
Aura of the Waters, Elías Huenún,
Catalina, Zulema, Carlos, Margarita,
my brothers and sisters named night after night
in the earth and the echo of lost mountains.

MARÍA ISABEL LARA MILLAPÁN

MANGIN

Mangituy ko
Tremtuy püyay ko
Ümawküley rayen
We küyen küpaltuy tami üy,
Welu ngelay tami pu nge,
Mawuni, mawuni
Mawün kimniey tañi rakiduam
Fey ñi piwke ka mapu müley.

MANGIN[125]

Bajo el agua
Duermen las flores en invierno
La luna nueva
Me trae tu nombre de regreso,
Pero no tus ojos
Llueve, llueve
La lluvia dice lo que pienso
Y mi corazón está lejos.

---

[125] Terreno bajo y húmedo, levemente pantanoso. También significa inundación.

MANGIN[126]

Under water
Flowers sleep in winter
The new moon
Brings your name back to me
But not your eyes
Rain, rain
The rain says what I think
And my heart is distant.

---

[126] Low and humid terrain, slightly swampy. Also means flooding.

RELMU

Tañi pu pewma amuley
Chew tañi chollüken relmu
Alofpakelu tañi rakiduam.

Nepen fey tañi piwke
Alküy tregül ñi ülkantun
Purulekelu mulfen kachu mew.

Pu trafia ülkantuy ngakiñ
Ponwitu foqui mew
Illiw ko püle,
Fey engün nga wuldungukenew
Pichi domo ngelu inche
Dewma inche mülen ñi ruka ñi kompellüm
Mew, pelolelu pu trafia ñi kütralwe mew.

RELMU[127]

Mis sueños van al lugar
Donde nacen los arco iris
Que alumbran mi memoria.

Despierto y mi corazón siente
El canto de los treiles[128],
Que danzan en la humedad del rocío.

Al atardecer cantan los ngakiñ[129]
Protegidos entre el boqui[130]
Allá en el estero,
Esos que cuando niña me respondían
Mientras yo esperaba su eco
En la puerta de mi ruka[131]
Alumbrada por el fogón del atardecer.

---

[127] Arcoiris.

[128] *Vanellus chilensis.* Ave conocida también con el nombre de *treile o tregle.* Se distribuye desde el valle de Copiapó hasta la isla de Chiloé. Los mapuches los consideran los guardianes de sus campos.

[129] Una especie de sapo.

[130] *Capsidium valdivianum.* Planta trepadora, siempre verde, de tallos delgados y prismáticos. Enredadera propia de los bosques nativos del sur de Chile. Los mapuches utilizan sus tallos par confeccionar todo tipo de cestas.

[131] La casa mapuche, hecha de madera, paja y barro.

RELMU[132]

My dreams return to the place
Where rainbows are born
Lighting my memory.

I wake and my heart feels
The song of the treiles[133],
Dancing in the dampness of the dew.

At dusk ngakiñ[134] sing
Protected by the boqui[135],
There in the stream
Where they returned my childhood call
While I waited for their echo
At the door of my ruka[136]
Lit by the evening fire.

---

[132] Rainbow.
[133] *Vanellus chilensis* (the Southern Lapwing, a large wader). A bird also known by the name *treile* or *tregle*. This bird is found from the Valley of Copiapó to the Island of Chiloé. The Mapuches consider this bird to be the guardian of their camps.
[134] A species of frog.
[135] *Capsidium valdivianum*. A climbing plant, evergreen, with thin, prismatic stems. Climbing plant native to the forests in the south of Chile. The Mapuches use its stems to make all types of basket.
[136] A Mapuche house, made of wood, straw and mud.

PEWMA

Anümka ñi rarakun
Lleniey üñüm ñi dungun,
Apon küyen
Niey tami rakiduam,
Puliwen tami llellipun
Pülef mawun mew,
Fey kürüf niey tami ülkantun
Inaltu lewfu püle.

PEWMA[137]

El susurro de los árboles
Tiene el mensaje de las aves,
La luna llena, tiene tu pensamiento,
El amanecer tus ruegos
En la llovizna, y el aire
Tu voz que canta a orillas del río.

---

[137] Sueño, soñar en términos generales. Los sueños son muy
importantes para los mapuches, ya que pueden contener elementos
y señales premonitorias. Por medio de ellos se puede también
establecer contacto o comunicación con lo sobrenatural. Para los
mapuches los sueños influyen directamente en la vida cotidiana.

PEWMA[138]

The whispering of the trees
Has the message of the birds,
The full moon has your thought,
And the dawn your prayers,
In the rain and the air
Your voice sings by the river.

---

[138] Dream, to dream in general terms. Dreams are very important
for Mapuches as they can contain premonitory elements and signs.
Through dreams contact can also be made with the supernatural. For
the Mapuches, dreams have a direct impact on daily life.

KINTU

Tripan ñi trekayal mawida püle
Ramtufin kürüf
Ñi elkünüken ñi dungun anümka mew,
Kiman rayüle folil
Pünchonule pewma,
Kiñetule taiñ dungun
Ka mapu elkenoelyinmew pu trafia.

Wiñotuayin may taiñ ülkantun mew,
Tripapale antü
Kayi choyüpe mawida
Fey dañeaiñ taiñ püllü,
Ka mongeaiñ
Inaltu lewfu
Dunguaiñ üñüm engo
Nütüaiñ taiñ tremolketuelchi tapül
Antü ñi kutran mew
Fewla inchiñ taiñ kidu ngetual.

KINTU[139]

He salido a caminar por las montañas
Y he preguntado al viento
Si guarda su voz entre los árboles
Entenderé cuando florezcan sus raíces
Y no se marchiten los sueños,
Cuando se unan nuestras palabras
Y no nos distancie la tarde.

Hemos de retornar entonces con nuestros cantos,
Cuando salga el sol,
Hemos de permitir germinar el bosque
Y anidar en la tierra nuestro espíritu,
Para volver a vivir cerca de los ríos
Hablar con las aves
Palpar las hojas que sanan el dolor del tiempo
Cuando queremos ser nosotros mismos.

---

[139] Palabra que hace referencia al sentido de la vista.

KINTU[140]

I have gone for a walk in the mountains
And I have asked the wind
If it hides its voice in the trees
I will understand when its roots flower
And dreams no longer wither away,
When our words unite
And evening can no longer distance us.

We will then return with our songs,
When the sun rises
We will allow the forest to germinate
And our spirits to nest in the Earth,
So we can return to live by the rivers
And speak with the birds
Touch the leaves that heal the pain of time
When we want to be ourselves.

---

[140] A word referring to the sense of sight.

INCHE TAÑI PEWMA

Inche tañi foye
Tañi pu küwü dipufi tami pu tapül
Wangülen ñi ñüküf mew.

Küyen ñi rüpü mew
Trafmenew tami pu folil, pilkach, rayen ka ngefün,
Fey trekan tami mongen mew
Tañi piwke ñi pu lemuntu püle.

FOYE[141] MÍO

Foye mío
Mis manos han alcanzado tus hojas
En el misterio de las estrellas.

En el camino de la luna
Me vinieron a encontrar tus raíces, ramas,
Flores y frutos,
Y caminé con tu vida
Hasta los bosques de mi corazón.

---

[141] *Canelo (Drimys winteri)*. Árbol sagrado del pueblo mapuche. Sus hojas y corteza poseen propiedades cicatrizantes y antibacterianas. Su corteza es rica en vitamina c y se le utiliza como eficaz remedio contra el escorbuto. Es útil para combatir el reumatismo, la sarna y la tiña y para limpiar heridas. En los últimos años se le han descubierto propiedades contra ciertos tipos de cáncer.

MY FOYE[142]

My foye
My hands have reached your leaves
In the mystery of stars.

In the path of the moon
Your roots, branches,
Flowers and fruit
Came to find me,
And I walked with your life
Towards the forests of my heart.

---

[142] *Canelo (Drimys winteri; Winter's Bark).* A sacred tree for the Mapuche people. Its leaves and bark have healing and antibacterial properties. The bark is rich in vitamin C and it is used as an effective remedy against scurvy. It is also used for combating rheumatism, scabies and ringworm and for cleaning wounds. In recent years, it has been discovered to have anti-cancer properties.

KOM PEWMA MEW

Kom antü felepeaymi may
Ka mapu feytachi rayen mew
Ka feytachi ko pewmaniekelumew eymi,
Ka üngümküli tami piwke
Tañi wiñoal inaltu alkütupallal
Mawidantu üñum ñi ülkantun
Dewma akulu pu trafia
Ñüküf mew duamtunielmew?

Kiñe antü
Küpallay ka wiñotuay küyen reke
Tami trekan,
Nüaymi kiñe pifüllka,
Fey puruaymi ñi dungun mew
Inaltu wall mapu;
Meli wallpa mew
Meli wallpa mew amuallin,
Alleay kürüf ka mawün,
Newentuleay taiñ pu che,
Wangülen engo küyen
Dunguafi kürüf.

Rüf dungu ngele taiñ ülkantun ka taiñ llellipun,
Llenieallin taiñ pu füchake che ñi püllu,
Fey wiñotuallin kidu engün reke,
Taiñ pewma mew.

EN TODOS LOS SUEÑOS

¿Siempre estarás
Lejos de estas flores
Y de estas aguas que te sueñan,
O esperará tu alma
Volver a escuchar desde cerca el canto
De las aves del bosque
Que al caer la tarde
En su silencio te recuerdan?

Algún día
Vendrán y volverán como la luna
Tus pasos,
Tomarás una pifülka[143]
Y danzarás con su sonido
Bordeando nuestro universo;
En cuatro giros
En cuatro vueltas iremos,
Nos sonreirá la brisa y la lluvia,
Irá tomando fuerza nuestro pueblo,
Las estrellas y la luna de nuestras banderas
Saludarán al viento.

Si nuestros cantos y nuestros ruegos son verdaderos,
Llevaremos el espíritu de nuestros abuelos,
Entonces volveremos a ser como ellos,
En la inmensidad de nuestros sueños.

---

[143] Instrumento musical mapuche, especie de silbato que produce un sonido monocorde. Se fabrican de madera y greda. Con la *püfilka* o *pifilka*, se imita el grito del ñandú que llama a sus crías.

IN ALL THE DREAMS

Will you always be far
From these flowers
And these waters that dream you,
Or will your soul wait to hear again
The song of the forest birds close by
That remember you in silence
At dusk?

One day
Your steps
Will come and return like the moon
You will take a pifülka[144]
And will dance with its sound
Bordering our universe;
In four revolutions
In four turns we will go,
The breeze and rain will smile at us
Our people will gain strength
The stars and moon of our flags
Will salute the wind.

If our songs and prayers are true,
We will carry the spirits of our ancestors,
Then we will be like them again,
In the immensity of our dreams.

---

[144] A Mapuche musical instrument, a type of whistle that produces a monochord sound. It is made from wood and clay. With the *püfilka* or *pifilka*, it is used to mimic the sound the nandu makes when calling its young.

ALIWEN

Ilkaluwan pu aliwen mew
Fey nütramkayan trukur engo
Ñi pelom trekan
Yeniey tañi pu che ñi dungun.

Ilkaluwan rangintu mawida ñi rayen mew,
Katruan kuyfi pewma, liftuan ñi rakiduam
Külon tapul engo.

ALIWEN[145]

Me refugiaré entre los árboles más antiguos
Y hablaré con la neblina,
Su paso visible e invisible
Tiene la imagen de lo sagrado de mi pueblo.

Me refugiaré entre las flores de la montaña,
Cortaré el lejano sueño y despejaré mi
Pensamiento con hojas de maqui[146].

---

[145] Árboles nativos de gran tamaño.
[146] *Aristotelia chilensis*. Árbol de 4 a 5 metros de alto de hojas
perennes. Su fruto, una baya pequeña y muy dulce, es comestible.
Los mapuches utilizan los frutos del maqui para preparar una bebida
alcohólica. El jugo de este fruto también se usa para teñir lana,
como febrífugo y como remedio contra enfermedades de garganta,
para curar heridas y para tratar ciertos tumores. El *maqui* es además
un árbol muy eficaz para controlar la erosión, ya que es la primera
especie que invade terrenos degradados.

ALIWEN[147]

I will seek refuge in the most ancient of trees
And converse with the mist
Its steps visible and invisible
Hold the image of the sacred for my people.

I will seek refuge among the mountain flowers,
I will cut the distant dream and clear my
Thoughts with maqui[148] leaves.

---

[147] Large native trees.
[148] *Aristotelia chilensis.* (Chilean Wineberry). A four or five metre high tree with perennial leaves. The fruit, a small and very sweet berry, is edible. The Mapuches use the fruits of the *maqui* to prepare an alcoholic beverage. The juice of the fruit is also used to dye wool, to reduce fever and as a remedy for throat illnesses, to cure wounds and to treat certain types of tumour. The *maqui* is also very effective in controlling erosion, being the first species to invade degraded lands.

PEWMAPEN

Feypipeyu ñuke,
kollküza pewmapen
meta küpalniepefin.
Feypipeyu tañi pire pewmapel,
txür inaltu foye,
eymi, tami metawe ko mew
alliwelen.

Witxamge tami zügu,
tami püllü ta ülkantuli.
Feytachi puliwen.
Tami zügu mew küpali pülef mawün
tami kallfü münu longko mew.

HE SOÑADO

Te he contado, madre
que he soñado con copihues[149]
trayéndolos en mis brazos.
Te he dicho que he soñado con la nieve,
juntas al lado del canelo,
tú con tu cántaro de agua que me sonríes.

Alza tus voces,
es tu alma que canta esta mañana.
Viene la llovizna con tu palabra
sobre tu paño azul.

---

[149] *Lapageria rosea*. Es una planta trepadora, de hermosa flor en forma de campana tubular y con colores que van desde el rojo al blanco. Crece en forma silvestre en bosques húmedos desde las regiones VIII a la X, aunque preferentemente en el siempre verde bosque costero valdiviano. Es la flor nacional de Chile. Los mapuches utilizan los tallos de esta planta en cestería y sus raíces para combatir enfermedades venéreas, contra la gota y el reumatismo. Su fruto es comestible.

I HAVE DREAMT

I have told you mother,
that I have dreamt of copihues[150]
carrying them in my arms.
I have told you I have dreamt of snow,
us together by the cinnamon tree,
you with your pitcher of water smiling at me.

Raise your voices,
it is your soul that sings this morning.
Drizzle comes with your word
on your blue cloth.

---

[150] *Lapageria rosea*. A climbing plant with a beautiful flower in the form of a tubular bell and with colours ranging from red to white. It grows wildly in humid forests from the eighth to the tenth region in Chile, although it prefers the Valdivian evergreen coastal woodlands. It is the national flower of Chile. The Mapuches use the stems of this plant in basket weaving and the roots are used for combating venereal disease, gout and rheumatism. The fruit is edible.

PEWKÜLEAYU

Amutuiñ nga lamgen kiñe antü
Fey eltuiñ ngaiñ küme mawida
Ka mapu ñi wurwur
Kiñe puliwen antü
Rupachi mawun mew
Ka püllay ko
Chew ñi ilkauken kürüf üñüm.

Pifuy nga ñi piwke
Tañi amual waiwen engo
Inaafiel rüpü
Elu temu ko püle.

Fewla fewla amutuy taiñ pu füchake che
Fewla wenu mapu ngetuyngün
Taiñ llellipun, taiñ rakiduam
Fewla fewla lamgen
Kidu taiñ dungun ngey.

PEWKÜLEAYU[151]

Hubo que partir un día, hermano
Y dejar el bosque perfumado
El vapor de la tierra
En una mañana de sol
Después de la lluvia
Y las lagunas donde suelen esconderse las aves del viento.

Cuánto habría dado mi corazón
Por cabalgar
Entre la brisa,
Y seguir las huellas
Que los frutos del temo[152]
Van dejando en el camino hasta el estero.

Ahora ahora los ancianos de mi tierra se están yendo
Ahora van sus ojos al wenu mapu[153]
Van sus ruegos, sus sentimientos,
Ahora ahora, hermano
Los encargados somos de llevar estos sueños.

---

[151] Forma protocolar de despedida. Significa "volveremos a encontrarnos".

[152] Temo o temu: *Blepharocalyx cruckshanksii*, un árbol de corteza rojo-anaranjada (también llamado "palo colorado"), infaltable en los esteros o terrenos húmedos, ya que hunde sus raíces en los cursos de agua permanentes. Puede alcanzar los 20 metros de altura y se extiende desde la V a la X Región de Chile.

[153] La Tierra de Arriba, lugar al que ascienden las almas de los mapuches fallecidos. Concepto que hace referencia al territorio donde habitan los antepasados y adonde llegarán los mapuches que no transgredan o alteren las leyes y el orden natural de las cosas. En este espacio espiritual los mapuches se transforman en halcones o cóndores del sol.

PEWKÜLEAYU[154]

I had to part one day, brother,
And leave the perfumed forest
The vapour of the earth
On a sunny morning
After the rain
And the lagoons where the birds of the wind would hide.

What my heart would have given
To ride
In the breeze,
And follow the tracks
That the fruits of the temo[155]
Leave on the path to the stream.

Now now the ancestors of my land are leaving
Now their eyes are going to the wenu mapu[156]
Their prayers go, their feelings,
Now now, my brother
We are the ones entrusted to carry these dreams.

---

[154] A protocol farewell. It means "we will meet again".

[155] Temo or temu: *Blepharocalyx cruckshanksii*, a tree with red or orange-coloured bark (also called "red stick"). The tree grows in water or it has its roots within a permanent water course. This corresponds to marshes, bogs, water courses, lake and river shores. It can reach 20 metres in height, and is found from the fifth to the tenth Region of Chile.

[156] The "Land of Above", the place where Mapuche souls ascend after death. A concept that refers to the land inhabited by the ancestors and the final destination of those Mapuches who do not transgress or alter the laws and the natural order of the universe. In this spiritual space the Mapuches metamorphose into falcons or condors of the sun.

OMAR HUENUQUEO HUAIQUINAO

CHI AYÜW

Kiñe üñüm ñi age mew
akuy antü tañi azkintutxipawe mew.

LA ALEGRÍA

En la pupila de un ave
llega el sol a mi ventana.

HAPPINESS

In the pupil of a bird
The sun arrives at my window.

ÑOCHI FEĻEN

Itxo zuamfiñ tüfeychi wanku
chew kiñechi
anüel
tañi ayüw.

PACIENCIA

Amo esa silla
donde alguna vez
se sentará
mi alegría.

PATIENCE

I love that chair
where one day
my happiness
will sit.

ALLUSH KÜRÜF

Fishkü mapu ka narfü.

Tüfamew pu aliwen müten
poyewafuygün.

LA BRISA

Tierra fresca y húmeda.

Aquí sólo los árboles pueden
enamorarse.

BREEZE

Fresh and humid earth.

Here only the trees
fall in love.

KÜREW

Pegelney ñi sheza chi kürew,
ñi luyüfün kurü takun,
ñi pu külog ge,
chi milla wayllil wente kümpey rüku,
ñi chozkelü kewün
üymekelu ta züllwimew.

TORDO

Luce su seda el tordo,
su lustroso traje negro,
los ojos de maqui[157],
la púa de oro sobre el pecho hinchado,
su lengua anaranjada
que se enciende para las lombrices.

---

[157] *Aristotelia chilensis*. Árbol de 4 a 5 metros de alto de hojas perennes. Su fruto, una baya pequeña y muy dulce, es comestible. Los mapuches utilizan los frutos del *maqui* para preparar una bebida alcohólica. El jugo de este fruto también se usa para teñir lana, como febrífugo y como remedio contra enfermedades de garganta, para curar heridas y para tratar ciertos tumores. El maqui es además un árbol muy eficaz para controlar la erosión, ya que es la primera especie que invade terrenos degradados.

THRUSH

The thrush flaunts his silky
lustrous black coat,
his eyes of maqui[158],
the tuft of gold on his puffed chest
his orange tongue
flickering out for worms.

---

[158] *Aristotelia chilensis.* (Chilean Wineberry). A four or five metre high tree with perennial leaves. The fruit, a small and very sweet berry, is edible. The Mapuches use the fruits of the *maqui* to prepare an alcoholic beverage. The juice of the fruit is also used to dye wool, to reduce fever and as a remedy for throat illnesses, to cure wounds and to treat certain types of tumour. The maqui is also very effective in controlling erosion, being the first species to invade degraded lands.

MAYKOÑO

Küme püchü mapu kono, ñimitufe, txapümfünüfe,
illpuymagelu maziwaza mollfüñ mew ñi pu kelüke namun;
añaz pilun ka itxo allküfe;
narfü müpü,llumfe, txemo;
chi kashü sheza pichuñ kuchulen
weñankü mew ka mawüza ñi küme nümün mew.
Pozkülen kachillantu ñi rügo mew
lelfün weñag azümküzawfe geymi.

Mawüzantü ñi karü am mew
ellkaneymi münche müpu tami zügulwe fey
    wümawtuleymi.

TÓRTOLA

Dulce palomita silvestre, recolectora, semillera,
untada con sangre de amapolas las rojizas patas;
oído delicado y descifrante;
alas húmedas, esquivas, gallardas;
el plumaje de seda gris mojado
con la tristeza y el perfume de los bosques.
Manchada con la harina del trigal
eres una artista melancólica del campo.

En el alma verde de la selva
escondes tu flauta bajo el ala y duermes.

TURTLEDOVE

Sweet, wild dove, collector of seeds
feet covered in the blood of poppies;
delicate and discerning ear,
moist wings, timid, gallant;
plumage of wet, grey silk
with the sadness and perfume of the forest.
Stained with the flour of wheat
you are a melancholic country artist.

In the green soul of the wood
you bury your flute beneath a wing and sleep.

KIÑE PÜCHÜ WENTXU INANEFILU ÑI PEWMA

Kiñe txitxag namun püchü wentxu gefüñ ge nielu
txanalen kiñe txunkuy mew,
gütxamkali üñüm egün
pirpirülelu manshanu mew.
Kiñe achawall ina lige karpümekey.
Chi püchü wentxu txekali epug mew tükunen ñi kuwü.
Gütxamkali püchüke achawall egun
fey elenufi afünke cereza;
gütxamkali pu aliwen egün
fey aye küme zuamüy.

UN NIÑO EN LA SENDA DE SU SUEÑO

Un niño descalzo con los ojos de avellana
tendido en una carreta,
conversa con los pájaros
que pían en el manzano.
Una gallina escarba cerca del lingue[159].
El niño camina con las manos en los bolsillos.
Conversa con los pollitos
y les convida cereza madura;
conversa con los árboles
y se complace sonriendo.

---

[159] *Persea lingue.* Árbol siempre verde que alcanza una altura de hasta 30 m y un diámetro de hasta 80 cm, corteza gruesa y rugosa de color café a cenicienta. Su madera se utiliza en mueblería y su corteza para teñir de café telas y lanas. Con sus frutos los mapuches fabrican una bebida alcohólica.

A CHILD IN THE PATH OF HIS DREAM

A barefoot child with hazelnut eyes
lying down in a cart
talks to the birds
chattering in the apple tree.
A hen scratches near the lingue[160].
The child walks with his hands in his pockets.
He talks to the chicks
and offers them ripe cherries;
he talks to the trees
and smiles, content.

---

[160] *Persea lingue.* An evergreen tree that grows to 30 metres with a diameter of up to 80cm, with thick, rough bark of a coffee to ashen colour. The wood is used in furniture making and the bark is used to dye cloth and wool a coffee colour. The Mapuches use its fruit to make an alcoholic beverage.

AFTÜKUN

Tüfa mülen,
wechuñ tüfachi lil mew
kiñe ñamku reke nielu epu mari txipantu
shikoniefilu ta kura
amelrakizuamkülen wüñotual
we txemkületuchi mawüza mew.

Faw chew gellu ella pegengelu
kiñeke waria ñi kiñeke allkütuwe ñi pañillwe müta.
Ellkawkülel münche pun ñi müpü mew
nawel ñi illku lemawenew
kiñe tapül reke kürüf ñi kuwü mew.

ABANDONO

Aquí estoy,
en lo alto de esta quebrada
como un águila de veinte años
que picotea una roca
con la visión de volver
al bosque rejuvenecido.

Aquí donde apenas es posible divisar
algunas antenas de radio de algunas ciudades.
Oculto bajo el ala de la noche
la fiereza del tigre se me fuga
como una hoja de las manos del viento.

ABANDONMENT

Here I am,
on top of this ravine
like a twenty-year-old eagle
that pecks at a rock
with the vision of returning
to the rejuvenated forest.

Here where you can hardly make out
some radio antennae from some cities.
Hidden beneath the wing of night
the ferocity of the tiger escapes me
like a leaf from the hands of the wind.

Steve Brock was born in Adelaide in 1971, where he lives with his wife and teenage daughter. In 1989 Steve lived in Argentina for a year on an AFS student exchange, and later majored in Spanish at Flinders University. He completed a PhD in contemporary Australian literature at Flinders in 2003. For the past decade Steve has worked in the public service as a speech writer and policy officer. He published his first collection of poetry *the night is a dying dog* in 2007 (Wakefield Press), and received a grant from Arts SA for the completion of *Double Glaze*, published by Five Islands Press in 2013. Steve is a co-translator of this anthology and has published his poetry translations from Spanish in a range of journals. His work featured in the *Best Australian Poems 2014* (Black Inc.).

Sergio Holas-Véliz was born in the port town of Valparaíso in Chile and migrated to Australia in 1988. He holds a Teacher of Spanish Degree, a Masters Degree in Hispanic Literatures, both by the Pontificia Universidad Católica de Valparaíso, and a PhD in Philosophy by The University of New South Wales. His poetry has been published in *Babab* (Spain), *Letralia* (Venezuela), *Arena* (Melbourne) and *Social Alternatives* (Queensland). He has published three poetry books: *Distancia cero* (Zero Distance; 2004), *Ciudad dividida* (Divided City; 2006) and *Paisajes en movimiento* (Moving Landscapes; 2013). He has taught Spanish Language and Latin American literature at Universidad Católica (Chile), Auckland University (New Zealand), Canberra University, Queensland University, Flinders University and is currently at the University of Adelaide. He is completing his first poetry book in English: *Adelaide, Ramblin' on My Mind: Meditation Upon Anomalies as Emergent Occasions*. He is a co-translator of this anthology.

Juan Garrido-Salgado was born in Chile and was a political prisoner under the Pinochet regime. He now lives in Adelaide. He has published three books of poetry, and his poems have been published in Chile, Colombia, Spain, El Salvador, Brazil, New Zealand and Australia. He has also translated into Spanish works from John Kinsella, Mike Ladd, Judith Beveridge, Dorothy Porter and MTC Cronin, including *Talking to Neruda's Questions*. He has translated five Aboriginal poets for *Espejo de Tierra/Earth Mirror Poetry Anthology*. He is a co-translator of this anthology. He has translated many of Lionel Fogarty's poems into Spanish. He is currently working on the Spanish translation of a selection of Jumoke Verissimo's poems to be read at the Granada International Poetry Festival in Nicaragua.

Víctor Cifuentes Palacios (1977) es poeta, músico, artista visual y traductor. Ha expuesto su obra pictórica en comunidades mapuches de la región de La Araucanía, Santiago de Chile, Argentina, Canadá y Francia. Como traductor ha colaborado en investigaciones académicas y diversos proyectos literarios, entre los que destaca su versión en mapuchezungun de *Epu Mari ülkantufe ta fachantü / 20 poetas mapuches contemporáneos* (Lom, 2003). Reside en la comunidad Santos Curinao de la localidad de Quintrilpe, comuna de Vilcún, Novena Región de Chile.

Víctor Cifuentes Palacios (1977) is a poet, musician, visual artist and translator. He has exhibited his art works in Mapuche communities in the Araucanía Region and Santiago, Chile, Argentina, Canada and France. As translator he has collaborated on academic research and a diverse range of literary projects, including his version in *Mapuchezungun Epu Mari ülkantufe ta fachantü / 20 poetas mapuches contemporáneos* (Lom, 2003). He lives in the Santas Curinao community in the Quintrilpe locality, Vilcún commune, Ninth Region of Chile.

Paulo Huirimilla Oyarzo nació en la isla de Calbuco (Décima Región de Chile) en 1973. Es profesor de Estado en Pedagogía en Castellano. Ha Publicado los libros *El Ojo de Vidrio* (2002), *Palimpsesto* (Lom Ediciones, 2005), *Cantos para niños de Chile* (Ulmapu Ediciones, 2005) y *Weichafechiül: cantos de guerrero. Antología de poesía política mapuche* (Lom Ediciones, 2012). Ha obtenido la beca del Consejo Nacional del Libro y la Cultura el año 2000 y los siguientes premios: "Juegos Literarios de Puerto Montt" (1997), premio "Edesio Alvarado" (1998) y el premio "Luis Oyarzún" (Valdivia 2001). Poemas de su autoría han sido incluidos en numerosas antologías, entre las que cabe destacar *20 poetas mapuches contemporáneos* (Lom Ediciones, 2003), *Cantares, nuevas voces de la poesía chilena* (Lom Ediciones, 2004) y *Los cantos ocultos: antología de la poesía indígena latinoamericana* (Lom Ediciones, 2008). Reside y trabaja en la ciudad de Puerto Montt. Mail de contacto: wirimilla@gmail.com

Paulo Huirimilla Oyarzo was born in the Isla de Calbuco (Tenth Region of Chile) in 1973. He works as a Spanish Professor and has published the books: *El Ojo de Vidrio* (2002), *Palimpsesto* (Lom

Ediciones, 2005), *Cantos para niños de Chile* (Ulmapu Ediciones, 2005) and *Weichafechiül: cantos de guerrero. Antología de poesía política mapuche* (Lom Ediciones, 2012). He won a National Council of Books and Culture fellowship in the year 2000, and the following prizes: "Juegos Literarios de Puerto Montt" (1997), the "Edesio Alvarado" prize (1998) and the "Luis Oyarzún" prize (Valdivia 2001). His poetry has featured in numerous anthologies, including: *20 poetas mapuches contemporáneos* (Lom Ediciones, 2003), *Cantares, nuevas voces de la poesía chilena* (Lom Ediciones, 2004) and *Los cantos ocultos: antología de la poesía indígena latinoamericana* (Lom Ediciones, 2008). He lives and works in the city of Puerto Montt. Email contact: wirimilla@gmail. com

Roxana Miranda Rupailaf nació en la ciudad de Osorno en 1982. Es profesora de Lengua Castellana y Comunicación. Ha publicado los libros *Tentaciones de Eva* (2003), *Seducción de los venenos* (Lom Ediciones, 2008) y *Shumpall* (Del Aire Ediciones, 2011). Recibió el premio literario "Luis Oyarzún" otorgado por el Gobierno de la Décima Región de Chile (2003) y el premio Municipal de Literatura de Santiago (2012). Productora del vídeo-poema *Shumpall* y antologada en "Epu mari ülkatufe ta fachantü: 20 poetas mapuche contemporáneos" (Lom Ediciones, 2003), entre otras antologías chilenas y latinoamericanas. Reside en Osorno. Mail de contacto: mirandarox@hotmail.com

Roxana Miranda Rupailaf was born in the city of Osorno in 1982. She is Professor of Spanish Language and Communication. She has published the books *Tentaciones de Eva* (2003), *Seducción de los venenos* (Lom Ediciones, 2008) and *Shumpall* (Del Aire Ediciones, 2011). She won the "Luis Oyarzún" literary prize awarded by the Government of the Tenth Region of Chile (2003) and the City of Santiago Literary Prize (2012). She is the producer of the video-poem *Shumpall* and has been anthologised in *Epu mari ülkatufe ta fachantü: 20 poetas mapuche contemporáneos* (Lom Ediciones, 2003), among other Chilean and Latin American anthologies. She lives in Osorno. Email contact: mirandarox@hotmail.com

Bernardo Colipán Filgueira nació en Osorno en 1967. Es profesor de Historia y Geografía, Licenciado en Educación y obtuvo una Maestría en Estudios Latino americanos en la Universidad Autónoma de México. Ha publicado *Pulotre: Testimonios de vida de una comunidad huilliche. 1900–1950* (Editorial Universidad de Santiago

1999), *Arco de Interrogaciones* (Lom Ediciones, 2005), *Forrahue: Memoria de una matanza* (2012), y *Comarcas* (2013), libro que recibió el Premio Regional de Poesía otorgado por el Gobierno de la Región de los Lagos. Es co-autor, junto a Jorge Velásquez, de *Zonas de Emergencia: Antología crítica de la poesía joven del sur de Chile* (Ediciones Paginadura, Valdivia, 1994). Recibió la Beca para Escritores del Consejo Nacional del Libro y la Lectura (1998) y la Beca de la Fundación Ford (2011). Su trabajo poético ha sido incluido en varias antologías de poesía mapuche y chilena. Reside en Osorno. Mail de contacto: likan37@gmail.com

Bernardo Colipán Filgueira was born in Osorno in 1967. He is a Professor of History and Geography, with a Bachelors Degree in Education and a Masters in Latin American Studies from the Universidad Autónoma de México. He has published *Pulotre: Testimonios de vida de una comunidad huilliche 1900–1950* (Editorial Universidad de Santiago 1999), *Arco de Interrogaciones* (Lom Ediciones, 2005), *Forrahue: Memoria de una matanza* (2012), and *Comarcas* (2013), a book that won the Regional Poetry Prize awarded by the Government of the Región de los Lagos. He is the co-author, with Jorge Velásquez, of *Zonas de Emergencia: Antología crítica de la poesía joven del sur de Chile* (Ediciones Paginadura, Valdivia, 1994). He won the Fellowship for Writers of the National Council of the Book and Reading (1998) and the Ford Foundation Scholarship (2011). His poetry has been published in a range of anthologies of Mapuche and Chilean poetry. He lives in Osorno. Email contact: likan37@gmail.com

María Isabel Lara Millapán nació en Freire, Región de la Araucanía, en 1979. Es académica del Departamento de Lenguaje del Campus Villarrica de la Pontificia Universidad Católica de Chile. Doctora en Didáctica de la Lengua y Literatura por la Universidad Autónoma de Barcelona. Sus líneas de trabajo se orientan en la didáctica de la lectoescritura, literatura infantil, literatura mapuche y enseñanza del idioma mapudungun. Ha publicado las obras poéticas *Puliwen ñi pewma / Sueños de un amanecer* (2002) y *Ale / Luz de la luna* (2012). Parte de su poesía se ha incluido en las antologías *Epu mari ülkantufe ta fachantü/20 poetas mapuches contemporáneos* (Lom Ediciones, 2003) y *La memoria iluminada: antología de poesía mapuche contemporánea* (Centro Editor de la Diputación de Málaga, España, 2007). Reside en Villarrica. Mail de contacto: mlaramillapan@gmail.com

María Isabel Lara Millapán was born in Freire, Región de la Araucanía, in 1979. She is an academic in the Department of Languages, Villarrica Campus, Pontificia Universidad Católica de Chile. She has a PhD in the Didactics of Language and Literature from the Universidad Autónoma de Barcelona. Her areas of work are orientated around the teaching of literacy, children's literature, Mapuche literature and the teaching of the Mapudungun language. She has published the poetry books *Puliwen ñi pewma / Sueños de un amanecer* (2002) and *Ale / Luz de la luna* (2012). Her poetry has been included in the anthologies *Epu mari ülkantufe ta fachantü/20 poetas mapuches contemporáneos* (Lom Ediciones, 2003) and *La memoria iluminada: antología de poesía mapuche contemporánea* (Centro Editor de la Diputación de Málaga, España, 2007). She lives in Villarrica. Email contact: mlaramillapan@gmail.com

Maribel Mora Curriao nació en Panguipulli, Región de los Ríos, en 1970. Cursó la carrera de Pedagogía en Castellano en la U. de la Frontera y es Magister en Literatura Hispanoamericana por la U. de Chile. Es co-autora del libro de relatos *El pozo negro y otros relatos mapuches* (Pewma Ediciones, 2001) y *recientemente publicó el libro de poesía* Perrimontun (Editorial Konünwenu, 2014). Poemas de su autoría han sido incluidos en las antologías *Sur Fugitivo: poesía joven de la Décima y Novena regiones* (Temuco, 2003), *Epu mari ülkantufe ta fachantü/20 poetas mapuches contemporáneos* (Lom Ediciones, 2003), *Hilando en la memoria* (Editorial Cuarto Propio, 2006) y *La memoria iluminada: antología de poesía mapuche contemporánea* (Centro Editor de la Diputación de Málaga, España, 2007). Parte de su poesía se ha traducido al inglés y al catalán. En la actualidad cursa el doctorado en Estudios Americanos en la U. de Santiago y trabaja en la U. de Chile. Mail de contacto. kurrimalen@gmail.com

Maribel Mora Curriao was born in Panguipulli, Región de los Ríos, in 1970. She studied Pedagogy in Spanish in the Universidad de la Frontera and has a Masters in Hispanoamerican Literature from the Universidad de Chile. She is the co-author of the book of short stories *El pozo negro y otros relatos mapuches* (Pewma Ediciones, 2001) and recently published the book of poetry *Perrimontun* (Editorial Konünwenu, 2014). Her poetry has featured in the anthologies *Sur Fugitivo: poesía joven de la Décima y Novena regiones* (Temuco, 2003), *Epu mari ülkantufe ta fachantü/20 poetas mapuches contemporáneos* (Lom Ediciones, 2003), *Hilando en la memoria* (Editorial Cuarto

Propio, 2006) and *La memoria iluminada: antología de poesía mapuche contemporánea* (Centro Editor de la Diputación de Málaga, España, 2007). Her poetry has been translated into English and Catalán. She is currently undertaking a PhD in American Studies in the Universidad de Santiago and works in the Universidad de Chile. Email contact: kurrimalen@gmail.com

Jaime Luis Huenún nació en Valdivia, Región de los Ríos, en 1967). Poeta y escritor mapuche-huilliche. Ha publicado los libros de poesía *Ceremonias* (Editorial de la U. de Santiago, 1999), *Puerto Trakl* (Lom Ediciones, 2001), *Port Trakl* (edición norteamericana de la editorial ActionBooks, Indiana, 2008), *Reducciones* (Lom Ediciones, 2012), *Porto Trakl* (edición italiana de la editorial *In forma di parole*, Bologna, Italia, 2013) y *Ko fenten püllu, mapu fentén püllu / Espíritu del agua y de la tierra: Teatro mapuche para niños* (Mineduc, 2013). También ha publicado las antologías *Epu mari ülkantufe ta fachantü/ 20 poetas mapuches contemporáneos* (Lom Ediciones, 2003), *La memoria iluminada: poesía mapuche contemporánea* (Cedma, Málaga, España, 2007), *Los cantos ocultos: poesía indígena latinoamericana contemporánea* (Lom Ediciones, 2008) y *Rayengey ti dungun/ La palabra es la flor: antología de poesía mapuche para niños* (Mineduc, 2011). Su poesía ha sido traducida al inglés, alemán, francés, holandés, italiano, catalán y francés. Ha sido invitado a lecturas y festivales poéticos en Estados Unidos, México, España, Argentina, Ecuador, Colombia, Perú, Nicaragua, Inglaterra, Irlanda y Alemania. Obtuvo el primer premio en el Concurso Nacional de Poesía "El joven Neruda" (Temuco, 1999); el Premio de Honor de la Ilustre Municipalidad de Santiago el año 2000; el Premio Pablo Neruda de Poesía otorgado por la Fundación homónima el año 2003. Se le otorgó la beca de la Fundación Guggenheim de Nueva York el año 2005. El Consejo Nacional del Libro y la Lectura otorgó el premio a la mejor obra poética editada en Chile a su libro *Reducciones* el año 2013. Hace clases en la Universidad Diego Portales de Santiago y dirige Ediciones Konünwenu, editorial indígena de Chile. Mail de contacto: wenunche@gmail.com

Jaime Luis Huenún was born in Valdivia, Región de los Ríos, in 1967. He is a Mapuche-Huilliche poet and writer. He has published the following books of poetry: *Ceremonias* (Editorial de la U. de Santiago, 1999), *Puerto Trakl* (Lom Ediciones, 2001), *Port Trakl* (edición norteamericana de la editorial ActionBooks, Indiana, 2008),

Reducciones (Lom Ediciones, 2012), *Porto Trakl* (Italian edition by the publisher *In forma di parole*, Bologna, Italia, 2013) and *Ko fenten püllu, mapu fentén püllu / Espíritus del agua y de la tierra: Teatro mapuche para niños* (Mineduc, 2013). He has also published the anthologies *Epu mari ülkantufe ta fachantü/ 20 poetas mapuches contemporáneos* (Lom Ediciones, 2003), *La memoria iluminada: poesía mapuche contemporánea* (Cedma, Málaga, España, 2007), *Los cantos ocultos: poesía indígena latinoamericana contemporánea* (Lom Ediciones, 2008) and *Rayengey ti dungun/ La palabra es la flor: antología de poesía mapuche para niños* (Mineduc, 2011). His poetry has been translated into English, German, French, Dutch, Italian and Catalán. He has been invited to readings and poetry festivals in the USA, Mexico, Spain, Argentina, Ecuador, Columbia, Peru, Nicaragua, England, Ireland and Germany. He won the inaugural Pablo Neruda Poetry Prize, presented by the Pablo Neruda Poetry Foundation in 2003. He won a Guggenheim Scholarship from New York in 2005. The National Council of the Book and Reading awarded him the prize for the best poetry book published in Chile for his book *Reducciones* in 2013. He teaches in the Universidad Diego Portales de Santagio and directs Ediciones Konünwenu, an Indigenous publishing house in Chile. Email contact: wenunche@gmail.com

Omar Huenuqueo Huaiquinao nació en 1971 en la localidad de Labranza, novena región de Chile. Poeta bilingüe autodidacta. Poemas de su autoría se han publicado en la revista *Pewma, Literatura y Arte* (1995) y en las antologías *Epu mari ülkantufe ta fachantü/20 poetas mapuches contemporáneos* (Lom Ediciones, 2003) y *La memoria iluminada* (Cedma, Málaga, España, 2007). Trabaja en faenas mineras en el Norte Grande de Chile.

Omar Huenuqueo Huaiquinao was born in 1971 in the Labranza locality, Ninth Region of Chile. He is a bilingual self-taught poet. His poetry has been published in the journal *Pewma, Literatura y Arte* (1995) and the anthologies *Epu mari ülkantufe ta fachantü/20 poetas mapuches contemporáneos* (Lom Ediciones, 2003) and *La memoria iluminada* (Cedma, Málaga, España, 2007). He works in mining operations in the Norte Grande (Big North) of Chile.